Building the Village

Collaboration Skills

for Educators and Nonprofit Leaders

Building the Village

Collaboration Skills
for Educators and Nonprofit Leaders

Hank Rubin, Ph.D.

**Foreword by U.S. Congressman Danny K. Davis
Introduction by Paul Houston, Ph.D.
Executive Director, American Association of School Administrators**

Chicago, Illinois

Published by
LYCEUM BOOKS, INC.
5758 S. Blackstone Ave.
Chicago, Illinois 60637
773/643-1903 (Fax)
773/643-1902 (Phone)
lyceum3@ibm.net

This book may be purchased at a substantial discount in bulk quantities. For information about bulk and individual purchases contact Lyceum Books.

Copyright © Hank Rubin, 1998

All rights reserved under International and Pan-American Copyright Conventions. No part of the publication may be reproduced, stored in a retrieval system, copied, or transmitted in any form or by any means without written permission from the publisher.

♦ ♦ ♦

A significant portion of proceeds from the sale of this book will be contributed to:

The Institute for Collaborative Leadership
202 South State Street
Suite 1302
Chicago, Illinois 60604-1905

Printed in the United States of America
February 1998

ISBN 0-925065-49-8

Dedication

To Elaine and Abraham Rubin who encouraged me to see the world through others' eyes. To Tina who bravely joined with me to build our little village. And to Amelia and Lane who joyfully inhabit it.

Hank Rubin
Chicago, Illinois
January 1998

TABLE OF CONTENTS

About the Author	ix
The Institute for Collaborative Leadership	x
Foreword by Congressman Danny K. Davis	xi
Preface and Overview	xiii
Introduction by Paul Houston	xix

1 Most of Us Begin by Missing the Point!   1

2 Collaboration: The New Frontier   5

3 Collaboration and Relationship Management   11
Why Is Collaboration Important? ♦ *Who Is a Collaborative Leader?*
What Distinguishes Collaborative Leaders from Other Types of Leaders?
From Semantics to Meaning ♦ *Time and Difference* ♦ *Time and Formality*
Itinerant Collaborations ♦ *Sustained Collaborations* ♦ *Veracity and Tenacity*
Conclusion: Collaborative Leaders Are Interinstitutional Organizers

4 Educators as Collaborative Leaders   25
The Case for Teachers as Collaborative Leaders
Creating a Learning Environment One-Relationship-At-A-Time
A Teachers' Review
The Easy Case for Principals and Superintendents as Collaborative Leaders

5 Building Collaboration: A 12-Step Process   35

6 The Dimensions of Collaborative Leadership   39

Psychosocial: Understanding People	41
Understanding the Rudiments of Each Sector	43
Diversity: A Process, Not an Outcome	46
Recruiting the Right Mix	48
Entrepreneurism	53
Charisma	60
Managerial Skill	63
Timing the Launch	65
Strategic Thinking	68
Group Process	71
Consensus Building	79
Professional Credibility	83
Integrity	86
Spirituality	89
Diplomacy	90
Marketing	94
Resource Development	95
Tenacity and Attention: Institutionalizing the Worry	96
Technological Savvy	99

7 A Few Nuggets   103

About the Author

Hank Rubin—founder and president of the Institute for Collaborative Leadership—grew up in Rochester, New York, in the shadow of the work of Saul Alinsky. That's where he was first exposed to the organizing principle of *seeing the world through the eyes of those you wish to influence.*

In a career that has spanned the sectors and ranged from national to local in scope—including service in the U.S. Department of Health, Education and Welfare, the Illinois State Board of Education and the Chicago Public Schools—Dr. Rubin has seen the world through the eyes of a broad cross-section of those who affect the quality of life of people living in America's large cities, particularly, urban children. He has taught 7th and 8th graders, run two nonprofits, created several others, directed and taught in the Midwest's largest urban graduate school of public (government and nonprofit) administration, served as vice president for sales and marketing in an international manufacturing firm, later served as associate vice president for institutional advancement in a large urban university, taught graduate students in education and business management, run for public office, and started and managed his own consulting firm.

Dr. Rubin has provided counsel and leadership to a variety of collaborative initiatives including the Chicago Panel on Public School Policy and Finance ("Chips"), the Community Service Management Program, a thriving Upward Bound coalition on Chicago's southwest side, the Bloomington-Normal Education Alliance, and the Access to Technology Resource Center serving Chicago's south side. He writes and speaks about relationship management with the intellectual clarity of a rigorously trained scholar and the practical and approachable credibility born of a career path that adheres to the organizing principle that propelled his career over twenty years ago.

Hank Rubin rose to national prominence in the academic study of nonprofit administration as convenor and co-chair of the Clarion Initiative (a series of symposia that began at Harvard's Kennedy School and were devoted to developing a consistent theory and target competencies to guide trainers and educators in developing curricula in nonprofit administration) and in the National Association of Schools of Public Affairs and Administration, where he was elected to leadership of the national section on nonprofit management before he left academe.

Through his consulting, lectures, and dozen-plus publications on topics including philanthropy, nonprofit management, ethics, school reform, and educational goal setting, Dr. Rubin is nationally recognized as an advocate for innovative and collaborative approaches to leadership, training and public education. In 1983, Dr. Rubin founded Rubin & Associates, a consulting firm dedicated to helping mission-driven nonprofit and education leaders develop the individual skills and collaborative opportunities to do their jobs better. R&A clients have included educational institutions and nonprofit organizations throughout the United States and overseas. In 1997, Dr. Rubin founded and became president of the Institute for Collaborative Leadership.

◆ ◆ ◆

Hank Rubin earned his doctorate from Northwestern University and his master's and bachelor's from the University of Chicago, with coursework at the State University of New York at Geneseo.

◆ ◆ ◆

The Institute for Collaborative Leadership

The Institute for Collaborative Leadership is a national nonprofit organization dedicated to promoting and enabling effective collaboration among people and the institutions they lead through research, training, teaching, technical assistance, advocacy, and publications.

Readers are encouraged to contact the Institute
for information about programs, services and membership.

The Institute for
Collaborative Leadership
202 South State Street
Suite 1302
Chicago, IL 60604-1905

randagroup@att.net
1/888/NPO-AIDE
phone: 773/743-0448
fax: 773/743-0440

FOREWORD

Nobody trying to get something done in the public sector can succeed by him or herself. Whether you are a teacher, superintendent, community activist, nonprofit leader, economic development administrator, philanthropic board member, or congressman, the fact is, if you don't know how to build effective and ongoing collaborative relationships with other people, you won't succeed.

I am delighted to have been asked to write this brief forward for Hank Rubin's new book <u>Collaboration Skills for Educators and Nonprofit Leaders</u>. This is the first in what will be a series of explorations of collaboration management by Hank and his colleagues at the Institute for Collaborative Leadership. With this book at the foundation, I think all of us who are toiling the soil of public service are in for some provocative, thoughtful, and very practical writings yet to come.

I've known Hank for more than a decade, since before the two of us were working to build the far-reaching coalitions that brought the late Mayor Harold Washington to power in Chicago. I later taught with Hank in Roosevelt University's Public Administration Program where I watched him assume national leadership in creating university programs for nonprofit administrators. Today, there are hundreds of university-based nonprofit management programs across the nation. I suspect that Hank is, once again, at the portal of a new area of university research and teaching. Lord knows, we need to understand, learn, and teach young and aspiring public leaders how to build and manage their relationships with other public leaders.

The book you are holding is important, practical and timely. This book is must read for any public leader. I challenge community leaders, educators at all levels, and political leaders to read this book and use it as a catalyst to fulfill the old African maxim: *It takes a whole village to raise a child.*

CONGRESSMAN DANNY K. DAVIS
U.S. HOUSE OF REPRESENTATIVES
7TH DISTRICT, ILLINOIS

PREFACE AND OVERVIEW

This is a brief book for people who dedicate their careers or volunteer their time trying to make a difference in public matters. It does not cull its management and leadership lessons from presidential campaigns, sports dynasties, dramatic corporate mergers, or public projects of the magnitude of the Tennessee Valley Authority or the Manhattan Project. Not that the concepts and skills we will discuss do not apply to these large complex operations; rather, these grand contexts are simply too distant to feel relevant for most of us who work and volunteer in the public sector. Besides, the size of institutions in which we operate has little bearing on the basic (human) relationship management skills that collaborative leaders must master in order to make a difference.

Therefore, this book is geared toward the familiar workaday world of public schools, local volunteer initiatives, and small and medium size nonprofits because these are the contexts in which most of us—practitioners and students—spend most of our time trying to get things done.

This is a book for teachers, educational leaders (in school districts and nonprofit and government agencies), staff members and volunteers in nonprofit organizations, and students preparing for any of these positions. It is a practical exploration of what it takes to form and focus the collaborative *relationships* necessary to accomplish important public missions like education. It is a book about *building villages*.

This edition is more a *book of concerns* than it is a *book of answers*. By trying to identify all the elements and steps that are part of collaboration, my aim is twofold:

1. To assist practitioners with models and provocations that will help them think about how to build and lead effective collaborations, and
2. To begin a dialogue that will generate more and more answers, models, and theories related to specific how-to questions facing practitioners and students.

Essentially, this book has two parts. Chapters 1-4 broadly establish the contexts of collaborations and pose a variety of arguments for *doing* collaboration. Chapter 5 outlines a simple 12-step conceptual model of the points to be considered as collaborations are built and managed. Chapter 6 is the workhorse, providing a series of short essays that explore the wide range of dimensions (characteristics and skill sets) of collaborative leaders. Finally, chapter 7 singles out a few essential characteristics of effective collaborative leaders for those readers looking for pithy guidance right away!

Building Relationships for Children

Because K-12 education is part of all our experiences—and part of the day-to-day lives of any of us with young children—nearly every reader will identify with this book's heavy focus on examples and discussion of *collaboration skills for educators*. As a nonprofit practitioner for over twenty years, I encourage my third sector colleagues to look for the relevance of our discussion of skills and principles to the work we each do as collaborative leaders in nonprofit organizations.

But the unabashed primary purpose of this book is to contribute to the art and science of collaborating in organized efforts to improve children's education.

Because *relationships* are at the core of collaboration, an easy case can be made that the most important public context for *doing* collaboration is in and around our public schools. *Building relationships between children and the institutions associated with schooling and learning is the most important and overlooked function of formal education.* The quality of that relationship—how good each child feels about his or her relationship with the institutions and individuals associated with education at the preschool and early elementary levels—shapes the educational self-concept, the formation of learning skills, and the educational goals of students. As students progress through the school system, this relationship affects dropout rates, individual career goals, and augurs each young adult's commitment to pursue the further schooling needed to make high career goals realistic.

Building relationships between schools and the public and community institutions that surround them is essential for the effectiveness and continued viability of both schools *and* community. It is reasonable to expect that the leadership for initiating, building and maintaining these relationships should come from education professionals. These are the people we trust and train to facilitate our children's growth into learned and learning young adults—but there are also wonderful examples in which this leadership stepped forward out of political and nonprofit positions.

A common phrase in education literature is "teacher as leader." This book will expand the conventional domain of school leaders (teachers, principals, and others) beyond the four walls of their classrooms or the borders of their school campuses to that of advocate and coalitional leader. Such leaders build collaborative relationships involving community organizations, social service agencies, government offices, political officials, philanthropies, businesses, parents, other school personnel, and children in order to meet the needs of children and families, serve the schools' instructional agenda, and, in so doing, improve the quality of life for the entire community.

Leaders of this type—in schools, nonprofits, and communities—are rare. But we know they're out there . . . and we need more of them. Where will they come from? (Keep in mind that the career paths of most school and nonprofit leaders have generally not wandered far from the four walls of schools and nonprofits very much like the ones they are now leading.) Where will they learn the skills? (To this date, there is no school, curriculum or degree in collaborative leadership.)

Teachers, school administrators, volunteers and nonprofit managers in youth-serving organizations and students preparing for any of these roles will find the discussion and lessons of this book most immediately applicable to their condition. College deans, university presidents, philanthropists, and government policy makers are in the best positions to carry this discussion forward so as to elevate collaboration as a priority of public leadership, integrate it into the training and certification of institutional leaders, and support the research and development that this emerging field logically deserves.

◆ ◆ ◆

First, Some Definitions

The jargon of new enterprises often gets in the way of effective communication of ideas. Let's begin, right away, by establishing some common sense definitions of key terms. We'll return to definitions in the body of this book in order to examine some concepts more deeply.

A *collaboration* is a purposeful relationship in which all parties strategically choose to cooperate in order to accomplish a shared outcome. Because of its voluntary nature, the success of a collaboration is dependent upon the ability of one or more *collaborative leaders* to build and maintain these relationships. *You are a collaborative leader* once you have accepted responsibility for building—or helping to ensure the success of—an interinstitutional partnership to accomplish a shared purpose. *Relationship management* is what a collaborative leader does: It is the purposeful exercise of behavior, communication, and organizational resources to affect the perspective, beliefs, and behaviors of another person (generally a *collaborative partner*) so as to influence his or her relationship with you and your collaborative enterprise. *Collaborative leadership is the skillful and mission-oriented management of relevant interinstitutional relationships.*

A Note to the Reader

Can we do this together?

This book begins a dialogue that should get each of us thinking about how to expand the scope of our visions, skills, and institutional resources so that building and contributing to successful collaborations becomes a routine part of how we do business. You and I are collaborators in this conversation!

If the first edition of this book succeeds in generating questions, comments, cases, and suggestions from you and other readers, then we will all benefit from the discussion that results. There is a comment form in the back of this book. Please use it: take a moment to share your thoughts as you read. Not only do I look forward to responding to your communications, but I promise that subsequent editions will be stronger and more helpful as a result.

If you can't find the comment form, please contact me via the Institute for Collaborative Leadership [202 South State Street, Suite 1302, Chicago, Illinois 60604-1905; 773/743-0448 (phone); 773/743-0440 (fax); randagroup@att.net (E-mail)].

Thanks.

HANK RUBIN
CHICAGO, ILLINOIS

INTRODUCTION

I met Hank Rubin several years ago after I spoke on a radio talk show in Chicago. Hank was listening to the program, liked what I said, and tracked me down. He was interested in working with the American Association of School Administrators (AASA). This is where collaboration starts: wanting, in a sincere way, to work together. Collaboration is more than the joining of parts: it is doing so in such a way that the venture becomes greater than the sum.

Since that time, Hank has become involved with AASA in helping the organization through some planning activities. He stayed in touch, and we have developed a healthy respect for each other and our work. In essence, we collaborated to make AASA better. Therefore, I was delighted to support Hank by joining the Institute for Collaborative Leadership's Board. I plan to offer insights from a national educational leader's perspective, and serving on the board will help me learn more about the new *basic skill* for leaders: collaboration. This, too, is a major part of what collaboration is all about, each gaining something from the other. It is not only what you take from the party, it is also what you bring to it. For our society to survive, we are all going to need to become better at collaboration, and leaders are going to have to get particularly good at it.

In discussions with school leaders, I have often reminded them that while takes a village to raise a child, the real question is "What does it take to raise village?" In fact, this is the central mission of school leaders as we stand poised the edge of the next millennium. Often communities are no longer examples common unity. They are divided in thought, fragmented in organization, and oft desperate in circumstance. They are in need of being wedded with a healing fabr of care and cooperation. The real challenge for leaders is not to lead nearly much as it is to help everyone else discover their own "inner leader" and to bler their energies and talents into a symbiotic symphony. The challenge is learning lead the orchestra. After all, conductors make no sound at all—they leave that the orchestra members. Leadership is not tooting your own horn, rather it is raisi a baton and helping the orchestra play together.

While leaders need to be courageous champions who stand up for childre and communities, they must also be collaborative catalysts who spark cooperatic and a sense of community. This idea poses a real shift from earlier models leadership. Today our society needs fewer "Lone Rangers" and more leaders of t posse. We need leaders who can blend their skills with those around ther Unfortunately, this is an emerging awareness, and too few are prepared to face t challenge.

<u>*Collaboration Skills for Educators and Nonprofit Leaders*</u> comes at a goc time. It offers insight into the key questions about collaboration and what might done to build relationships that support children and communities. It provides a understanding of what collaboration is and what it is not—what its elements a and how to get there. It moves you from a basic overview of the need for, and t concept of, collaboration to a deeper understanding of what collaboration is, wt it is important, and how you might create it. For that reason, this is a helpful boc

d one that breaks new and important ground in the struggle for creating collaboration so that we can begin to build our villages once again.

PAUL HOUSTON, EXECUTIVE DIRECTOR
AMERICAN ASSOCIATION OF SCHOOL ADMINISTRATORS
ARLINGTON, VIRGINIA

CHAPTER 1

|MOST OF US BEGIN BY MISSING THE POINT!|

All but a very small handful of colleges of education miss the point. Scarcely any of the emerging academic programs preparing nonprofit administrators have gotten it. But community organizers have almost always practiced it.

The general public knows the point when it sees it . . . and knows it more acutely when it's absent.

"It" is the respect, humility, trustworthiness, interpersonal and organizational skills, credibility, and focused self-discipline that enable a regular person or a public leader to build and sustain the relationships that are necessary to get a job done in public. The public careers of many smart people have risen and fallen on the steep inclines of their superior intellect, oratory, attractiveness, energy, and vision. But without the skills of relationship management (or astute hiring of these skills in a close and effective advisor), their public profiles are unstable or short-lived.

Many people with good intentions and high energy set their hearts on accomplishing some public good but stumble, ultimately, and throw in the towel. They fail, most often, because they never learned the skills of building the collaborative base of support and workers that is usually necessary in order to transform dreams into practical and sustainable initiatives. For public leaders and regular people, alike, there are few places to turn to acquire these skills.

Project LEARN in Los Angeles has developed an effective routine for building sustainable local coalitions that broaden the base of support for principals and teachers in their work on behalf of children. Communities in Schools and Colin Powell's *America First* have raised the profile of school-community collaboration on the national agenda. The School of Education at Washington University in St. Louis appears to be teaching future educators the imperative of becoming community leaders on behalf of their students. The Anne E. Casey Foundation provided national leadership by funding research and programs to foster "systems integration": the practice of engaging local parks, libraries, social service providers, and other institutions in collaborative planning, budgeting, and service provision with schools so that whole villages may, in fact, raise the children. And, more recently, the Amherst H. Wilder Foundation has contributed relevant and helpful publications for nonprofit leaders.

There are more examples, coast-to-coast, in which thoughtful practitioners and thinkers are nibbling at the imperatives and outcomes of effective *collaboration* and *relationship management*. What's missing is (1) a clear and common vision of what it takes to be an effective collaborative leader and (2) a curriculum—or, at least, a series of outcome measures—that can be used to teach someone to be one. This book lays a foundation for the discussion and research that are part of curriculum development.

CHAPTER 2

COLLABORATION: THE NEW FRONTIER

Several years ago, when I was directing the school of Public Administration at Roosevelt University, I discovered the phrase "If you can make a difference, then you have a responsibility to do so." During twenty-plus years of work with education and nonprofit organizations, I've grown convinced that this philanthropic temperament is behind nearly every teacher, street corner activist, volunteer board member, literacy tutor, March-of-Dimes canvasser, community organization administrator, school principal, and leader who has ever tried to change a piece of his or her world. With all this good intention, why don't we see more good being accomplished?

Americans today share an overwhelming cynicism about public service that can be traced to the gap between good intentions and failed or twisted outcomes. Over 150 years ago, the great French social observer Alexis de Tocqueville raved of the unique emerging character of our then-young nation:

> These Americans are the most peculiar people in the world. You'll not believe it when I tell you how they behave. In a local community in their country a citizen may conceive of some need which is not being met. What does he do? He goes across the street and discusses it with his neighbor. Then what happens? A committee comes into existence and then the committee begins functioning on behalf of that need, and you won't believe this but it's true. All of this is done without reference to any bureaucrat. All of this is done by the private citizens on their own initiative.
>
> Americans of all ages, all conditions, and all dispositions consistently form associations . . . to give entertainments, to found seminaries, to build inns, to construct churches, to diffuse books . . . (<u>Democracy in America</u>, 1862)

Today, there's no simple and direct line connecting the identification of a need, the convening of a committee of peers, and the fulfillment of that need . . . I'm not sure there ever was. Politicians, regulations, daycare problems, second jobs, pervasive apathy, and hundreds of other complicating variables intercede between intentions and outcomes.

Even with technology that allows for instantaneous communication, getting things done in public remains a difficult and complex ambition that still relies on one neighbor's fundamental ability to build, nurture, and focus human relationships. In the 1960's and 70's, we came to call this *organizing*. Our search for understanding led us to learn that organizing entails a body of professional skills and an artistic temperament that was best codified and taught by Saul Alinsky, the father of modern social organizing. Alinsky was a prolific and idiosyncratic writer and trainer whose books and training programs shepherded a generation of labor organizers, civil rights organizers, community organizers, and others onto the streets to change a piece of the world. His *Rules for Radicals* was the blueprint for neighborhood leaders and movement strategists working to mobilize people so as to influence those in power.

In the 1980's and early 90's, the focus turned to managing the social service, arts and culture, health care, economic development, and myriad other nonprofit organizations that exist to accomplish important public missions. It was no longer enough to simply light passionate fires in the hearts of mission-driven people by organizing them; now we demanded that our leaders have the skills to stoke and nurture those fires and focus their heat by managing the organizations that exist to accomplish these public missions. Total Quality Management (TQM), Re-Engineering, and other high-profile management trends (which, I will argue, amount to little more than Alinsky's key principles polished to remove their contentiousness and outfitted in suits and ties for corporate consumption) led the nation into an era of management. Academicians of a certain stripe throughout the nation struggled to build curricula in nonprofit administration spearheaded by prominent sector leaders at Independent Sector, by progressive philanthropies like the Kellogg Foundation, and by intellectual enterprises like the Clarion Initiative (which drew together scores of scholars and practitioners at Harvard's Kennedy School of Government to begin shaping the academic discipline of nonprofit administration by differentiating it from business and government administration). Technical assistance providers like the Support Centers and Executive Service Corps worked to professionalize nonprofit managers by providing for their training and professional development needs.

Now we look forward to a twenty-first century in which technology will further shrink our global village. But, in those private moments of candor, nearly every expert agrees that we have no idea at all just how, for example, technology, demographics, the continued erosion of public confidence in public schooling, transformative issues such as charter schools and vouchers, and the notoriously thinning pool of able candidates for superintendencies will change the face of public education *just ten years from now.* Nor can we predict the human and societal implications of welfare reform, of global warming, or even the more distant—yet still influential—implications of the breakup of the Soviet Union. We are at no shortage of public issues around which passionate organizing can occur, yet this is an era curiously devoid of public passion.

The idealism that propelled our radicalism and organizing short decades ago is replaced by family-centered pragmatism in the baby boomers as we reach middle age and by cynicism among the Generation Xers whose age would otherwise suggest idealism. We are chary of social evangelists yet supportive of entrepreneurism. We are opposed to big government yet demanding of new solutions for long-standing social problems. We are demanding more of our nongovernmental social safety net, yet, as individuals, we are giving less. The solution to these ironies, we are told by foundations and government granting agencies, lies in partnerships, connections, alliances, collaborations.

In the fields of education, social service, health care, and the arts, collaboration offers the advantage of moving us beyond our *toolbox mentality*: a mentality that has us building the capacities of our organizations in order to accomplish their specific missions by identifying and mastering a prescribed set of tools we think our missions demand. The metaphorical adage, *when your only tool is a hammer, you tend to see all your problems as nails,* sheds light on the limitations of this approach. Collaborations not only add tools to the toolbox, they add diversity to the perspectives, broaden our understanding of the problems, and multiply the stakeholders with vested interest in seeing that our mission-driven goals are met.

Collaborations also go a long way toward resolving a common and unattractive characteristic of both public and private institutions: the common tendency to become so vested in the success of a *single best solution* (ours) or the priority of a *single most important issue* (ours) that we compete in the marketplace rather than looking there to find colleagues who can help us solve the underlying problem. The inherently competitive nature of both the private and public sectors—in which we all see ourselves as battling for a share of the same limited resources—establishes us as competitors with prospective partners, doing battle with them to elevate our competitive positions and, in so doing, to disprove their ideas, to diminish their importance, to undermine their strivings. This is an inherent inefficiency of the marketplace for which collaborative leaders are the solution.

◆ ◆ ◆

We are entering the age of collaboration: a new frontier, a child of organizing and management. This era demands of its practitioners interinstitutional organizing (dependent upon the interpersonal skills needed to build and sustain effective relationships) and principled institutional leadership (wherein the principles of sound management are firmly in place before one organization reaches out to partner with another). And, because collaborations are the vehicles for those of us who believe *we can make a difference*, this era marks the nexus of pragmatic outcomes-oriented management and public-spirited idealism. Above all else, collaborations exist to accomplish tangible outcomes, changing a little piece of the world every time we succeed.

CHAPTER 3

COLLABORATION AND RELATIONSHIP MANAGEMENT

WHY IS COLLABORATION IMPORTANT?

The problems and needs confronting our communities are far too complex for unilateral action and independent actors, no matter how well intentioned. It's become cliché to note that it takes a whole village to raise a child; but, make no mistake about it, the successful public leaders of the twenty-first century will be those most skilled at building villages.

Ultimately, democracy demands it. By removing peerage and legalized class differences from civil society, democracy makes each citizen equally powerful—or powerless—in terms of impacting everything from federal laws to local school budgets. To accomplish change in democracy and civil society, the effective leader amasses power—one individual or one institution at a time—until enough has been gathered to crest the barriers and accomplish the goal. In a very real sense, collaboration is democracy's mandate.

We tried big government and learned that it can't solve our problems by itself; the private sector shouldn't; and schools and nonprofits (separately, and in the many combinations we've tried) haven't. If our education and social service problems are to be solved, our arts and culture preserved, the health and quality of life improved, then we must set about building, nurturing, and managing new combinations—new *collaborations*.

Not convinced? Then ask yourself: Why do so many schools, nonprofits, and philanthropies fail to make the difference they dreamed of making? It's not for lack of good intentions: Schools and nonprofits attract mission-driven people—intrinsic-types who fervently want to make an impact. And it's not for lack of a good sense of what needs to be done. Schools and nonprofits attract professionals and volunteers who are at least as knowledgeable in their fields as are folks working in business and government agencies.

They fail, in large measure, because getting things done in public *always* entails collaboration and too many public leaders never learned how to build, sustain, and direct relationships with the people and organizations with whom they must collaborate.

The very structure of schools and nonprofits demands these collaborative skills of its leaders. In this regard we are very different from individual entrepreneurs (who can often tuck in their chins and plow ahead without regard for collaborative relationships) and corporate moguls (who can build homogenous systems beneath them to accomplish their goals):

- Our policy boards are richly diverse collections of agendas and people out of which we must build shared visions, goals and collaborative teams.
- The constituencies we serve are never really homogenous, even though they may share significant characteristics in common.
- We are increasingly pushed toward interinstitutional collaboration by the growing belief that meeting the education, health care, cultural development, and human service needs of children, families and communities requires a comprehensive and integrated approach that can be accomplished only through cooperative relationships with other providers.
- The culture of education and nonprofits—along with the comparative limitations of our economic resources—puts pressure on our leaders to recruit and engage volunteers for their minds, talents and access to resources.
- Our reliance on outside funders necessitates strategic alliances appealing to the institutional self-interests of diverse agencies and donors.
- And our responsibilities to educate the diverse public and offer positive direction to elected policy makers necessitate far-reaching and ever-changing strategic alliances.

Leaders of public organizations so often fail to achieve their original visions because they and their colleagues fail to recognize the importance of collaboration, because collaboration is more time consuming and challenging than is acting on one's own; because collaboration requires skills they were never taught, and because a collaborative way of thinking, in some very real ways, conflicts with the traditional structures and reward systems in which they routinely work. So we all have found ourselves trying to avoid collaboration, diminishing its central importance, doing it poorly, or defensively dismissing it as an external mandate—something we do simply because funders tell us we must. This is a big mistake.

The challenge before each of us who assumes a position of public leadership is to become an agent for collaboration and to develop the skills that will enable us to support and become collaborative leaders for the twenty-first century.

Who Is a Collaborative Leader?

The moment you decide to contribute to the success of a collaborative enterprise, you are a collaborative leader! There is nothing esoteric or remote about this concept; it is quite simple. Once you find yourself in a position to convene a collaboration or to be convened as a partner in another's collaborative initiative, then your realm of influence and leadership has expanded to include individuals and institutional representatives in leadership posts within other organizations. This makes you a colleague of these leaders, and a leader in your own right. This is true if you are a teacher convening the program directors from the local library and park district to plan an integrated program on astronomy for your seventh graders, a superintendent at the table with the chamber of commerce and economic development commission, or a single mother building a support network of social service providers and GED trainers for a sustained campaign to lift other women in your neighborhood out of the cycle of welfare dependency and into self-confident and permanent employment.[1]

The difference between a *collaborative leader* and a *collaborative partner* is a difference of volition. One chooses to play either a proactive or participatory role in the collaboration. And, just as many teachers have mastered the art of teaching from the back of the classroom, one doesn't need to be the convenor nor a routinely vocal participant during meetings to play a leadership role in strategically moving a collaboration toward its stated mission.

As a rule, only one or two members of a collaboration will take the time to think about how to move the collaboration forward and keep the collaboration alive. This is the central job of the collaborative leader. In this role, you and I will spend most of our time running the maze of interpersonal and interinstitutional politics that are necessary to build and sustain the interest and involvement of each collaborative partner. Assuming that it is in the interest of the collaboration's mission to engage the full array of partners in the discussion and process of planning and executing the work of the collaboration, this too is the job of the collaborative leader. The effective collaborative leader, therefore, finds a way to engage each partner individually by attaching the work of the collaboration to that partner's individual or institutional self-interests.

---

[1] Note that collaborative leaders live in the village (either the physical or professional community) they are trying to build. It's not unusual for outside experts to be brought in in order to bridge differences, help strategize operations, or facilitate the group's process; but these outsiders are *collaborative facilitators*, not collaborative leaders.

What Distinguishes Collaborative Leaders from Other Types of Leaders?

Collaborative leaders are interpersonal and interinstitutional relationship managers.

In public, we get things done *with* and *through* people. An effective public leader doesn't so much "lead" as he or she builds, sustains and directs the commitment, skills, and attention of followers and collaborators (just as a good teacher doesn't "teach" so much as she or he builds and nurtures the relationship of each child to the resources, skills, and personnel associated with learning and schooling). Relationships are the vehicles through which we accomplish the purposes for which we have developed our skills; *collaborations are purposeful institutional relationships.* It's worth repeating that our many levels of interdependence are part of what differentiates the public from the private sector. Unlike the private sector, those of us in the public sector are mistaken if we believe that we can succeed in some public action by simply attaching our blinders and plowing ahead. Without building and coalescing our partnerships, we will fail to do what's needed in order to succeed.

Institutional relationships are particularly complicated because they work (or don't work) at two levels: (1) They operate through the personalities and egos of the organizations' leaders and (2) They impact each organization's individual culture, programs, identity, and relationships with funders.

From Semantics to Meaning

The types and labels of collaborations we build will vary, but their dependence on our well-honed skills of relationship management will be constant. As we work to transform the still-young art of collaboration management into a teachable science, the now nearly-interchangeable terms "coalition", "collaboration", "alliance" and "partnership" will take on separate meanings:

- One term will certainly be elevated to represent the ideal of *cultural transformation in which shared visions and interinstitutional cooperation are the norm*,
- Another term will undoubtedly be chosen to represent long-term institutional relationships created when the scarcity of resources threatens the independent survival of the now-interdependent agencies,
- Another may come to stand for the short-term tactical relationships that are aimed at producing some immediately measurable outcome.

Some institutions, such as the venerable Industrial Areas Foundation (IAF), aim for the ideal of cultural transformation. They recognize that getting things done with and through collegial organizations really means getting things done with and through the people who run the organizations. They aim for the most fundamental marriage of self-interests and joint action by working slowly, methodically, and one-on-one to engage leaders emotionally (almost spiritually) in a common vision. Where the leaders go, it's reasoned, the organizations will follow.

Most of us will be less thorough than the IAF. But, to be effective, we will need to be equally as attentive to the human element. During the year I spent building the Chicago Panel on Public School Policy and Finance (a coalition of diverse civic organizations convened in the mid 1980's), a bit more than half of my time was spent drafting and refining the coalition's mission and operating procedures so as to meaningfully support the program goals, mission, and operating practices of each prospective member and funder. The rest of my time was spent building relationships of trust and collegiality so that each prospective member and funder could be confident that this initiative would be worth their investment.

There are two lessons here:

> 1. Institutional relationships succeed only insofar as the structures and procedural practices of the coalition are compatible with those of its member organizations.
>
> 2. Institutional relationships succeed only insofar as individual relationships are effective.

The ability to build and sustain relationships at both the individual and institutional level—and the ability to find common self-interests in the diverse missions and goals of independent organizations—defines the effective collaborative public leader.

Time and Difference

By this time, we have pretty much dismissed semantics and scale as making much of a difference in our new conversation about collaborative leadership. Now let's take a look at the role that duration plays in a collaborative initiative.

CHAPTER 3

Time and Formality

In general, the only differences between complex collaborations (that make big demands on their members) and small focused collaborations (that we easily roll in and out of) are *time* and *formality*.

Within collaborations, formality is a function of time. Let's examine this assertion:

Goals that require short low-maintenance collaborative engagements require few managerial structures and, therefore, can be accomplished with few or no rules and a great deal of informality. Complex goals that can be accomplished only via some sustained operation over time, require operating rules, maintenance systems, budgets, and greater formality.

Most collaborative leaders and partners are under pressure to be as efficient as possible in the time they spend on collaboration business. Most are so constantly mindful of their institutional and individual self-interests that they want to spend as much time as possible on producing the outcomes that the collaboration was convened to accomplish, and *as little as possible on process*. As a result, there is an inherent reluctance to spend time building formal infrastructures, except when the goals of the collaboration could not be accomplished without them.

Itinerant Collaborations

All of us have entered into short-term, or *itinerant*, collaborations in which a number of individuals and institutional representatives convene to tackle specific, clearly defined, and quickly achievable outcomes. We pass in and out of itinerant collaborations just as easily as the tide ebbs and flows; we convene, focus our energies, struggle with obstacles, accomplish our purposes (hopefully), then go our separate ways. When another collaborative need arises we have a pool of colleagues from which we draw collaborative partners and around whom we build the collaboration. The unique agenda, problem, or need being addressed will define who we optimally want around the table each time we build an itinerant collaboration.

Nonetheless, because we
1. get better at this the more collaborations we build,
2. are inclined to look for routines and patterns that will simplify our lives, and
3. usually find that it is easier to adapt and stretch existing relationships than it is to build new ones,

our second, third, and later itinerant collaborations are likely to end up looking like *roundups of the usual suspects*, predictable cliques of individuals and institutional representatives who work well and accomplish goals together. There is nothing wrong with this, if it works. And, if it works, then we are on our way to evolving our itinerant collaborations into a long-term *sustained* collaboration.

Sustained Collaborations

These are planned and managed systems of ongoing interaction involving individuals and institutional representatives for whom participation in the collaboration is essentially part of their job descriptions. Sustained collaborations are strategic, purposeful, high-maintenance efforts, whether they evolve from a series of effective itinerant collaborations or emerge whole-cloth as new entities. Their missions are either complex or long-term, with flexible goals, and maintenance costs. As noted above, the simple fact that sustained collaborations must last awhile demands strategic planning, flexibility, and management systems that require formality and structure.

Veracity and Tenacity

There is one more regard in which the issue of *how long a collaboration must last in order to accomplish its goal(s)* can make a difference: The longer the spotlight shines on the character of the collaborative leader, the more the success of that collaboration depends on the quality of that character.

Veracity. An inauthentic collaborative leader, like a loveless lover, may be able to put on a convincing performance for a brief time but will ultimately be brought down by the truth. Countless short-term collaborations have been built in order to highlight and glorify one organization. Countless have been built so that one "lead organization" could justify its application for funding. But while these may portray themselves as collaborations—even succeed in selling themselves as collaborations—these are not collaborations, they are *endorsements*. Weakly skilled collaborative leaders can call in debts and recruit partners from admiring friends, but these collaborations will work only for the short-term, until personal and institutional demands draw friends and colleagues away or until they grow tired of the convenor's inability to produce anything in the collaboration that fulfills their self-interests.

Tenacity. In the context of collaboration, the key to tenacity is perpetual attention and adaptation to the evolving contexts and self-interests of each collaborative partner. It is the difference between shooting a photograph versus a motion picture, capturing an image in a momentary relationship versus capturing and sustaining a relationship over time.

Conclusion: Collaborative Leaders Are Interinstitutional Organizers

Short-term collaborations designed to accomplish some immediate and visible outcome (for example, to engage the park district and museum in a middle school science curriculum or to influence legislation) are relatively easy to build. They are reactive, time-limited, and highly focused. To build this coalition all one has to do is convince each partner that (1) their individual and institutional self-interests will be served by it and (2) the instructional program or law is more likely to be accomplished collaboratively than independently. The value of this collaboration is that it produces a meaningful product, is great practice for building a more complex and sustained collaboration, and strengthens the personal relationships between leaders of collaborating partners. In classic organizing terms, small successes are organizing tools around which collaborative partners can be reconvened and expanded.

In general, the purpose of convening longer term coalitions is to advance a particular agenda more effectively than individual organizations can do independently. Whether the agenda is meaningful experimentation with varied approaches to education (such as may be offered by charter schools), community economic development (like Community Development Corporations), cultural transformation (such as IAF), or something grander yet (like the United Nations), the challenge is to build both a collaborative vision and relationships that are clearly and consistently compatible and

Chapter 3

important vis-a-vis the evolving missions, practices, self-interests, and leadership of the collaboration's members.

An exercise reportedly used in Saul Alinsky's training program for community organizers put the virtues of building short-term and long-term alliances in a meaningful context. Trainees were asked: If your goal is to organize a community so that it develops leadership and vision that will enable it to solve its own problems, which of the following problems would you tackle first?

1. The neighborhood's infestation of rats that are biting and poisoning children on the streets and in their homes, or
2. The need for a stop sign on a street corner that everyone knows is dangerous, where accidents and near-accidents happen almost daily.

The answer is the more immediately achievable and visible accomplishment of getting a stop sign installed. Once the stop sign is erected, it will stand as a source of pride, a symbol of what can be accomplished in coalition, a rallying point for future collaboration . . . a tool that the organizer can use to build the skills, relationships, confidence, and vision needed to attack the more complicated tasks of eradicating rats and leading a community.

◆ ◆ ◆

Much of what this book discusses is descriptive of leaders in general. What distinguishes the focus of this discussion is the attention paid to the *interinstitutional dimensions* of leadership, the dimensions that reach across the borders of institutions to engage individuals and organizations in collaborative efforts. The focus is on more than just how to get people to want to follow us into battle; it is on the strategies and tools that are needed to bring diverse individuals and diverse institutions to a table in order to develop the relationships necessary to accomplish a purpose that would otherwise be unattainable by any one individual or institution. These are the skills that neighbors need in order to organize a park cleanup, that social service administrators need in order to develop new programs with their staff and board members, that teachers need in order to build a successful dropout prevention program, that cancer society solicitors need in order to cultivate sustained givers, that religious leaders need in order to lead and follow their boards of directors, that parents need in order to make a difference in their schools and communities . . . skills that enable activists, community leaders, school administrators, teachers, nonprofit volunteers, arts administrators, and (even) elected officials do their jobs better.

This is organizing at the interinstitutional level. And whereas community and labor organizers are trained to patiently build their movements through one-on-one conversations with each individual they want to recruit, we as collaborative leaders build our movements one institutional relationship at a time, with the often repeated caveat that collaborative relationships happen at both the individual and institutional levels.

The added burden of building and sustaining *institutional* relationships means that we must have all the interpersonal skills of other leaders and organizers along with the administrative know-how of running institutions and knowledge of how other institutions and leaders, in other sectors, operate.

CHAPTER 4

EDUCATORS AS COLLABORATIVE LEADERS

THE CASE FOR TEACHERS AS COLLABORATIVE LEADERS:
Creating a Learning Environment One Relationship at a Time

In the cool objectivity of reflection, was your formal education a good experience?

Chances are, all else being equal, if your answer is *yes* you've gone on to pursue the educational credentials necessary for the career you've dreamed of or the job you realistically expect to achieve, and you owe a big "thank you" to one or more of your teachers. If your answer is *no,* then, in all probability, you're stuck without the educational qualifications you think are necessary for the job you want to be in, and you never had a teacher who married your dreams to your ambition to learn.

Whether you are rich or poor, your *perception* of the quality of your prior school experience—how *good* you feel about the quality, relevance and rewards of the schooling you've received—may be the best predictor of whether or not you *choose* to continue your education and certainly is the best predictor of whether or not you *desire* to continue with it.

With computers in preschools; impersonal and decaying large urban school districts straddling politics, financial ruin, low test scores, and high dropout rates; the escalating battle between schools and the streets (or the malls) for control of the educational agenda for our children; and the easy isolation offered by television and video games that mollify and transport youngsters away from learning relationships—the *human* truth of formal education remains: much like eating clams or holding hands, if you feel *rewarded* by what came before, you are much more likely to choose to do it some more.

This is the fundamental behavioral truth of relationship building: We are drawn, and return, to that which is rewarding. All these years, we have been concentrating on reading, writing, and arithmetic (and, more progressively, logic, literary awareness, and creativity) as the essential products of elementary and secondary education. But, while these are certainly important outcomes of public schooling, they are the *primary outcomes* only for those *consumers* (students) who choose to stop their education at or before high school graduation.

For everyone else, these studies are the elemental *tools of the trade*—the things that teachers do with us and to us as we work together to shape our individual senses of our capabilities, self-worth, and prospective futures in education. These studies are our individual primers; intended to be the first things—not the last things—we set out to learn. The purpose of good education is not only to teach us the primers, but to teach us *how to learn* them . . . *and to want to learn more.* When education succeeds in this way for a student, it's almost always due in large part to a teacher who made the connection work.

The focus of the good teacher is on process even more than content; all grown-ups remember the tone, attitude, and respect of our favorite teacher(s) much more than the topics she or he covered in class. We remember how that teacher made us feel about ourselves within the learning environment. These teachers were collaborative leaders, drawing us into a shared vision of learning as a rewarding lifelong effort: a loftier and longer term goal than that of most collaborative leaders.

Teachers, as the primary agents of education, play the largest role in shaping and controlling the effectiveness of students' relationships with their learning environments and the process of learning. Good teachers translate the complex and often competing demands we place on them into individual strategies for connecting learners to learning. You will find many of these same demands (and strategies) at work in the United Nations, at labor/management bargaining tables, at condominium board meetings, and in economic development commissions.

We expect these relationships to be productive in the eyes of all the parties involved. We expect them to be measurably related to a meaningfully larger purpose. We expect the time we spend together to be well planned, pleasurable, and efficiently productive. We expect all parties to make their best contributions to the success of our relationship. These expectations are the sum and substance of *relationship management:* the art and science of building and sustaining the relationships necessary to get things done. For a good teacher, relationship management entails building, nurturing, and instilling a relationship between each student and his or her education in which the *relationship* is viewed as pleasurable, important, challenging, and meaningful in the mind of the student.

For children growing up in poverty, the role of teachers in shaping educational self-worth is especially important since, to these children, teachers may be the only flesh-and-blood purveyors of school-like education and models of educational achievement. They are the truth-telling evaluators of educational *"fit"* (both judging and influencing whether students find comfort, fulfillment, and the tools to succeed in an educational environment). For these children, teachers, especially early elementary teachers, have been found to play an even larger role than do mothers in influencing students' long-term educational aspirations.

In a world of international trade and competition, the effectiveness of our teachers as collaborative leaders takes on national importance: There can be no more important education or economic priority for this country than to keep our children going to school for as long as it takes for them to learn what they need in order to acquire the credentials they will need to have a realistic shot at the professional goals they will set for themselves. Short of chaining our children to their desks, the only way we will make this happen is by increasing their *desire* to complete their secondary schooling and to pursue postsecondary education. We count on our teachers to build the relationships that instill this desire.

As America's corporate sector settles into its age of managerial enlightenment (learning, at last, through TQM, Re-Engineering and the like that businesses succeed through relationships and not growth models and robotic production lines), the new goal of every sales, marketing, and customer service department is to build relationships with their customers of such trust and loyalty, in which the needs of each customer are so well projected and met, and in which buying from the company is so comfortable and rewarding that every customer will desire to do it again and again regardless of the product's price. Students who find education comfortable and appropriately rewarding are bound to want (and more likely to pursue) more of it, no matter how hard they individually find the schoolwork to be. Students (first) and their families (second) are the most important client-partners of our public education systems. Their relationships with our schools will not be strengthened by reduced expectations, comfortable fluff, or classroom candy. They will be strengthened when we shift the way we institutionally relate to them from a *parental model* to an *enlightened consumer model*, an approach to public education that treats students and their families as collaborative partners in a mutually productive relationship.

The question is, how *do we increase the desire of our consumers, our students, to seek continued education?* The answers lie, in part, in (1) the demanding challenge of restructuring *early* education so as to lay the groundwork for these relationships *right off the bat* and (2) developing training, incentives, and accountability for all educators so as to raise the priority of relationship management at all levels of education and for all of schooling's constituencies.

This will demand no less than a reconsideration of, first, how our colleges of education prepare our future educators and, second, the priorities that we, as a nation, set for funding and evaluating elementary and secondary education. Each factor will influence the success of the other.

As educators and as a nation, our focus must be on more than the substantive outcomes of elementary and secondary education. *Relationship management* should be a priority, at the center of how we recruit, prepare and certify educators. And it should shape what we expect—and how we measure the effectiveness—of our teachers and school administrators. How we prepare them, how we evaluate them, and the status we afford them should be centered on their ability to develop and nurture, *one at a time*, the relationships that will ensure a generation of committed learners.

A Teachers' Review

Collaborative leaders are interpersonal and interinstitutional relationship managers. Isn't it time we thought of elementary and secondary teachers in this capacity? Educators in the twenty-first century will need to be skilled, creative and collaborative community leaders on behalf of the learning needs of children and their families. This is a larger role than is conventionally implied by the phrase "teachers as leaders" and pertains to more than the centrally important relationships teachers will develop and manage with the students in their charge.

Teachers in the twenty-first century will be village builders. Through conventional and computer-assisted means, they will connect with a universe of people and resources. They will convene the social service providers whose services will help ensure that their students can learn and their families can promote children's learning. They will build relationships with corporations, philanthropists, and government agencies that will augment their limited resources so that children can succeed. They will develop partnerships with other public institutions such as libraries, parks, and police districts, and private interests such as chambers of commerce and local banks so that services and programs can be coordinated and communities can be organized to support specific developmental needs of children and their families.

THE EASY CASE FOR PRINCIPALS AND SUPERINTENDENTS AS COLLABORATIVE LEADERS

We don't need to break through as many preconceptions and stereotypes to agree that we expect principals and superintendents to be leaders. Because all of us were once children and many of us have children, we know that we need our educational administrators to understand their role, and function effectively, as *educational* leaders much more than as simply *school* leaders: more so community-wide advocates, mentors and convenors; less so site-based managers and regulators.

The distinction is this: *Education* is a *process* to which we all must contribute. *Schools* are *buildings*, simply places where this process occurs.

This is an important distinction that Paul Houston, president of the American Association of School Administrators, draws very well: The effective leaders of the twenty-first century will be **superintendents of education**, not *superintendents of schools*. They will be community leaders operating on behalf of the instructional and learning needs of children and their families. They will rally the resources, prick the consciences, and focus the energy of individuals and institutions from every sector of their communities so as to educate their children. They will be boundary-spanning advocates and administrators for whom *"the schools"* will be only one locus of their work. They will be measured far less by the effectiveness and efficiency of the administration of their buildings and staffs and far more by their ability to rally and sustain the devoted attention and resources of their entire community in relationships that meaningfully enhance the educational achievements of their students (perhaps reflected, one day, by the things those students accomplish long after they have left formal education).[2] The same will be expected of principals.

They will be collaborative leaders. Follow the workday schedule of superintendents and principals today, and you will find that many already are.

Superintendents and principals have three influential constituencies: their school boards or local school councils, their teaching and nonteaching staffs, and the individuals and institutions in their communities. Superintendents and principals are the conduits, catalysts, and executors for ensuring that education reflects the will of the board, the skill of the teachers, and the best investment of the entire community. This challenge, which is almost never without conflicting self-interests between competing constituencies, is the most compelling collaborational responsibility of educational leaders.

In their larger context, the universe of prospective collaborative partners for principals and superintendents includes individuals and administrative units on their staffs as well as individuals and institutions from across their districts, from other parts of their states, and in model

---

[2] Many of the ideas and perspectives offered in this section were influenced during a retreat of the senior staff of the American Association of School Administrators held November 1996. The author facilitated that retreat and is indebted to Dr. Houston and his entire Executive Team.

districts and professional associations throughout the nation. Their role, as collaborative leaders, involves convening—and supporting the convening by others—of the variety of individual and institutional resources that will collaborate in order to accomplish targeted objectives that will improve educational outcomes.[3]

Superintendents and principals have the same collaborative leadership responsibilities that the first section of this chapter spells out for all educators . . . but, not only do they have a larger territory, they have the added generic and routine collaborative responsibilities vis-a-vis school board, staff, and community, But perhaps their most important collaborative job is to create an environment within their schools and districts that supports and encourages every educator to provide this collaborative leadership.

◆ ◆ ◆

The rest of this book focuses on the concept of relationship management and the skills and principles of effective collaborative leadership. More than for any other constituency, this is a book for teachers, other student service personnel, principals, superintendents, and the sphere of nonprofit and community leaders whose missions and work revolve around building villages of support to raise children.

---

[3] In Bloomington-Normal Illinois, the president of Illinois State University convened the superintendents of the community's two school districts and the president of the local community college to create the Bloomington-Normal Education Alliance, a collaboration that may well be the nation's only ongoing proactive school-college coalition. With no crisis to react to or looming problems to solve, all four education agencies are working to translate optimistic visions of the future of education in this community into initiatives and programs that are likely to succeed.

CHAPTER 5

BUILDING COLLABORATION: A 12-STEP PROCESS

What do we need to consider as we build and manage collaborations? There is a genius to the simple and practical 12-step systems that have become the hallmark of self-help traditions and personal empowerment programs: They stretch our thinking to the limits of what our minds can realistically hold onto at any given moment, and they give us a protocol for ordering our action and planning. Let's try to do this here, as a first step in looking at just what it takes to *do* collaboration.[4] *(If you do it differently, let me know . . . especially if it works!)*

---

[4] Note that these steps are not a linear sequence (with each step following and depending on the one preceding it). Several of the steps are overlapping and may occur simultaneously.

The series of brief essays that follow in Chapter 6 explore the various skills and principles that you and I should understand and employ as we proceed through these steps and set out to become more effective collaborative leaders.

THE 12-STEP PLAN

Step 1: Figure out what you really want to achieve. Reduce the problem(s) you wish to solve or the vision you hope to accomplish to its most potent lever: the action or achievement that will have the greatest impact on your goals. Be very clear on the question of how and why a collaborative approach improves the likelihood of accomplishing your goals.

Step 2: Identify the outcomes you are targeting and the turnkey decision makers who must be influenced in order to accomplish your desired outcomes.

Step 3: Identify the full range of essential stakeholders and recruit a strategic core of them into the collaboration.

Step 4: Frame the issue so as to *(a)* solidify the connection of partners' self-interests with the mission and operation of the collaboration (and, thereby, build and reinforce their commitment to the collaboration) and *(b)* be able to tell the rest of the world just what it is the collaboration is (or will be) doing.

Step 5: Select the collaboration's leaders, formalize roles, and develop ground rules for the operation of the collaboration (including method and frequency of internal communications).

Step 6: Develop an *action plan* for the collaboration that creatively and efficiently maximizes the contributions of each collaborative partner to the collaboration.

Step 7: The *action plan* should begin by targeting successes around either the most urgent or the least controversial elements or goals and should incrementally build upon successes toward greater and more complex achievements.

Step 8: Efficiently and effectively implement the action plan.

Step 9: Build the essential bond between collaborative partners, create an internal environment of trust, loyalty, and high professionalism early on so that, later on, partners will be willing to make the compromises demanded in the context of collaborative decision-making.

Step 10: Celebrate the collaboration's successes with *internal recognitions* so as to strengthen the bond and raise the floor beneath the capacity and vision of the collaboration; and with *external publicity* so as to build momentum around the mission and success of the collaboration.

Step 11: Find creative and effective ways to routinely measure, adjust, and reinforce the bonds between collaborative partners in the collaboration.

Step 12: Revisit the mission of the collaboration, especially at significant benchmarks or when changes in external conditions affect the collaboration. Be flexible enough to explore the pros and cons of all the options you may have, including: *(a)* Modifying the mission and/or operating ground rules, *(b)* Retaining them intact, *(c)* Expanding or redirecting the mission, or *(d)* Taking a vacation or disbanding.

CHAPTER 6

THE DIMENSIONS OF COLLABORATIVE LEADERSHIP

Collaborative leaders, like the collaborations they help lead, are nearly always greater than the sum of their parts. Because of the synergy of their diverse dimensions, effective collaborative leaders stand out as visionaries, challenging thinkers, and people with whom others like to associate. Arrogance, insensitivity, self-aggrandizement, and the like are barriers to collaboration; people don't want to roll up their sleeves to join in and work along side any of these characteristics.

The following dimensions are the personal tools that collaborative leaders can use to accomplish collaboration. In the *ideal* world, all these dimensions combine in the sainted leader whom we follow into the jaws of collaboration. In the *real* world, they exist to varying degrees: Our very human leaders are certain to be missing several of these dimensions. For most of us, these are the *ideals* toward which we aspire as we strive to improve our abilities to build and lead collaborative initiatives. To become effective collaborative leaders, we need both mastery of those dimensions that are irreducibly essential along with an ability to compensate for absent dimensions by educating ourselves and by developing and sustaining close leadership relationships with collaborative partners who have and contribute the missing skills.

It is important to affirm here that collaborative leadership is a body of skills and characteristics that *can be learned*. Max DePree, in his book, <u>Leadership Jazz</u> (New York: Dell 1992), draws ample parallels between institutional leaders and jazz musicians who master the basics of their own instruments, practice with their group, and learn the strengths and weaknesses of their musical partners, all so that they might improvise together.

The remainder of this book is devoted to discussions that introduce the dimensions of (or skill sets that comprise) collaborative leadership. They are the starting points for self-assessment by collaborative leaders, targets for self-improvement, skills that we will look for in the partners we aim to recruit into our collaborations. At the same time, they constitute an outline of the competencies around which we may begin to build curricula for teaching the skills of collaborative leadership.

DIMENSION

Psychosocial: Understanding People

The most elemental skill required of collaborative leaders is the interpersonal skill and empathy needed to make and sustain strong linkages between the *people* who represent the institutional partners.

While collaborations generally link *institutions*, the institutional decision to join is made by *individuals*. And, as each institutional partner chooses the person who will represent them in the collaboration, it is the commitment and style of that selected representative that will define the quality and influence of each institution's participation.

At the very foundation of effective collaborative leadership (and of nearly any type of leadership, for that matter) is the interpersonal skill and empathy needed to make and sustain strong linkages between *people*. The tools begin with a built-in radar that detects the personal self-interests people bring into a relationship, that deduces each person's level of commitment to the relationship, and that observes and interprets the relevant psychosocial rhythms and styles of the individual. Effective leaders, in any context, understand the character, needs, work styles, capacities, and self-interests of the people they work with.

This leadership challenge is more complicated for collaborative leaders because we are not simply dealing with individuals as complex psychosocial organisms, we are dealing with individuals as complex psychosocial organisms *and* as representatives of complex institutions with highly individualized structures, needs, histories, and institutional self-interests.

Collaborative partners connect with the collaboration at two levels:

The first is at the level of *mission*. In the individual, this is the "must have" attachment, an affiliation that one is compelled to have because it is either *(a)* So obviously attached to the spiritual or professional identity of the individual that it is inconceivable (or would be terribly embarrassing) that this person would not affiliate or *(b)* In the institutional interest of an organization that delegates its affiliation to an individual representative. *This is what brings individuals to the collaboration table in the first place.*

The second is at the level of the *individual needs*. This is the dimension that grows from the collaborative leader's effectiveness at getting the individual feeling good and well rewarded by his or her involvement in the collaboration. *This is what determines the level of energy and engagement each individual exercises in the collaboration.*

As collaborative leaders, we are always aware that people representing institutions within a collaboration are regularly balancing what they would *like* to do—taking the positions and making the decisions that would satisfy their own personal self-interests—with what they know they *should* do in their representational capacity—taking positions and making decisions that serve their institutions' best interests. This is a constant internal negotiation in which an institutional representative may be just as likely to sacrifice a particular self-interest in order to meet an institutional need as she or he is to take action that would serve a self-interest if it can be rationalized by mildly stretching and interpreting their institution's interests. Effective collaborative leaders know that collaborative partners interpret (if not shape) their institutions' interests in the collaboration.

DIMENSION

Understanding the Rudiments of Each Sector

Effective collaborative leaders not only reach beyond the limits of their own organizations, they reach across professions and across the boundaries that define the nonprofit, government and for-profit sectors. Most of us need to expand our limited knowledge of others' professions and the other sectors so as to be able to find mutual self-interests, to build effective relationships, and to understand the conditions that affect the decisions and needs of our collaborative partners.

To be effective collaborative leaders, we don't need to be expert in the legal, social, historical and cultural elements of the professions, organizations, and sectors from which our collaborative colleagues come. But we do need working insights so as to be knowledgeable of the institutional contexts that shape our partners' interests and perspectives as they work in the collaboration for two reasons:

1. In a manner of speaking, we need to be able to look through the eyes of our colleagues so as to see ourselves and our collaboration as each collaborative partner sees us.
2. We need to be sensitive regarding the culture, ethos, and needs of the professions and organizations that our colleagues represent so as to engage and respond to them with understanding and respect.

Seeing the world through our colleagues' eyes (point 1, above) is a parallel skill to understanding our partners' self-interests: Both are essential if we are to successfully engage them in our collaboration and make their participation productive. Institutional representatives see us as a vehicle for accomplishing something for their institutions: We need to know what that is. Moreover, not only do institutional representatives carry into the collaboration specific goals from their home institutions, they come too with policies, politics, reporting relationships, time frames for getting things done, and other influences from their home institutions that shape what they expect from, how they view, and how they operate within the collaboration. Here's a simple illustration of what some of these differences might be:

Partners who come from entrepreneurial for-profit businesses, where decisions are made quickly on the basis of clear-cut bottom-line criteria, may be most comfortable in a collaborative environment that is fast-paced, formal, quantitative . . . and that meets at 6:00 a.m. before the workday begins. Partners coming from education and nonprofit institutions, where decisions are often participatory and broad based or where the criteria for making and evaluating decisions are less clear-cut, may attach themselves with more conviction to collaborations that tap and stroke their affective connection to people and missions . . . and that begin at 5:30 p.m., just before their round of late-night community meetings.

The respect that is borne of knowledge about others and their contexts (point 2, above) is a vital element of this dimension. We respect people who respect us. And no right-minded person would willingly volunteer to follow a collaborative leader whose behavior or lack of knowledge suggested disrespect. But, in the stereotypic shorthand to which we all fall victim, educators and nonprofit people have little respect for the self-serving ruthlessness of business people, business people have little respect for the mushy soft-headedness of soft-hearted educators and nonprofit people, and no one has respect for the heartlessness and blundering inefficiency of government bureaucrats. As someone who has been all three, I promise any doubters that these stereotypes are no more true of the other sectors than they are of yours.

It should go without saying that effective collaborative leaders can never permit themselves to fall victim to this sloppy world view. But almost every year the fundamental disrespect of some significant leader is exposed by a hidden microphone or video camera that captures a slur, an epithet, or a demeaning joke. We ridicule leaders who inappropriately stereotype and demean people because of what they do for a living just as we attack leaders who expose themselves as racist, sexist, or otherwise bigoted. This is the way it should be.

DIMENSION

Diversity: A Process, Not an Outcome

Diversity is not an accomplishment (that is, reaching recruitment and employment percentages that reflect the demographic makeup of a target market), it is a process. Collaborations that don't reflect the diversity of their constituencies in the context of America's sweeping demographic transformation run the immediate and fatal risk of being illegitimate, unresponsive, or worse.

Effective collaborative leaders are adept at spanning boundaries of every type—between sectors, genders, races, religions, ethnicities, and preferences—in order to bring together those who will be affected by and those who can influence the goals of the collaboration. We should make no mistake: The demographic trends of our nation project that, to an increasing degree, there is scarcely a public issue worth working on that will not affect diverse constituencies or be controlled by decision makers who do not look or speak like you or me.

A legacy of the last forty years is that *legitimate* leadership exists in *every* identifiable demographic group. There is no need to resort to window dressing; every earnest collaborative leader can find someone within (by that I mean *part of*) any target population who can represent that population in the collaboration with credibility.[5] To effectively recruit and engage diverse partners in the collaboration, we need to understand the historical and cultural conditions that influence each (prospective) partner: We need to be able to see ourselves and our collaborative issues through the eyes of diverse *"others"* .But, while this raises all the same concerns as discussed in the previous Dimension and calls for the same cautions, self-education and respect, it also calls for more.

To be credible, a collaboration must include, respect, and engage at equal levels representatives from all constituencies affected by the collaborative issue. This level of inclusion, respect and equity does not have precedent in every community. In many cases, we will be reaching across racial, religious, and ethnic lines in ways that have not been done before, and our outreach may not always be trusted or well received. In the context of this discussion of diversity, we have the added duty of building relationships (where none might have been before) with patience, tenacity, and initial focus on those irreducibly common concerns and needs that are important to diverse leaders (central elements of a *collective* self-interest) and that will assure such leaders that there is good reason for them to sit at a table with us.

---

[5] While this is irrefutably true, in the ghettos of many of our large cities it is made increasingly complicated by the dwindling number of legitimate institutions that can support institutional leaders and by the rise of (what some have called here in Chicago) *"professional ethnics"* who make their livings representing their understanding of the needs of their communities. Because there are many legitimate leaders in these communities who either do not have institutions which may serve as their base or the skills and experience to build such institutions, the *Institute for Collaborative Leadership* has initiated Startup Management Services (SUMS) to help legitimate leaders in these communities translate important ideas and social visions into incorporated and viable nonprofit agencies. With these agencies as their base, these leaders become not just credible, but identifiable and available collaborative partners.

As collaborative leaders, we have the additional mandate: to examine our own prejudices and stereotypes so as not to be mastered by them, but to master them.

We grow, as collaborative leaders, by learning to see the world through the eyes, traditions, values, and sensibilities of the people around us. This is not simply an idle liberal world view, it is a practical body of knowledge that makes public leaders more effective.

DIMENSION

Recruiting the Right Mix

Nothing shapes the culture, process, and outcomes of a collaborative initiative as much as decisions related to who is asked to join the collaboration.

The universe of prospective partners in our collaborations draws principally from two sources:

1. All the individuals and institutions in positions to make *turnkey decisions* that may affect the accomplishment of a part or the whole of the collaborative purpose.
2. All individuals and institutions with an historic or contemporary *stake* in the outcome of the collaboration's venture.

(As you move through the following discussion, keep in mind that narrowing down this universe and recruiting your collaborative partners will get easier as your knowledge and involvement in other institutions grow, as your networks of institutional leaders expand, and as more and more institutional leaders see your collaborative leadership as a resource for the accomplishment of their goals.)

Our ability to identify *turnkey decision makers* is wholly dependent upon our ability to break down our collaborative purpose into the steps and stages that will require action and decisions. Then our success rests on some basic research questions:

> ➤ Where (in what institution) does the authority reside to take a needed action or make a critical decision?
> ➤ Who within that institution has the authority to make that decision?
> ➤ What individuals and conditions affect this decision maker? (This raises the issue of webs of influence. It also calls on us to make a prediction of just how important public relations and media relations are likely to be in accomplishing the collaboration's targeted outcomes.)
> ➤ What resources (financial; managerial, including maintaining and managing the collaboration; political; etc.) are likely to be needed in order to accomplish the collaboration's intended outcomes?

The answers to these questions will produce a pool of turnkey decision makers and individuals who have the capacity to influence these decision makers. Once we've prioritized this pool and set our sights on prospective partners, our challenge is to work through all *"seven degrees of separation"* to ascertain how close we can come to communicating directly (or indirectly) with our targeted prospects, and then to develop our strategies for reaching them.

To build a pool of *stakeholders* in our collaborative purpose, our question is: What other individuals and institutions have a history and stake in the issue or outcomes we are pursuing? This is both an *historical* and *survey* question:

> ➢ What other organizations and individuals would benefit directly or indirectly from the work of the collaboration?
> ➢ Are there organizations and individuals whose knowledge of either the issues or the decision makers command their participation in the collaborative venture?
> ➢ Are there organizations and individuals whose reputation and prestige would either improve the collaboration's capacity to influence decision makers, other stakeholders or constituencies—or who would be especially notable in their absence?
> ➢ Are there organizations and individuals with sufficient history related to the collaborative purpose that their absence from the collaboration would signal (or suggest) a purposeful break with them?
> ➢ Are there organizations and individuals who could work compatibly and productively within the collaboration and whose involvement would somehow reduce or obviate certain known opposition to the collaboration?

There is another linear progression of events that may take place within the process of collaboration building. It is the science and art of identifying, recruiting, convening, and leading the *core group* of collaborative partners around whom the collaboration's membership and action plan may be built. [For small or short-term *(itinerant)* collaborations, there generally is no distinction between a *core group* and the *full membership* of the collaboration.] If done carefully, this can be the stimulating and rewarding phase during which the dream and vision of one person or organization takes shape, is bolstered by a new collective wisdom and power, and becomes larger than it had been before. If done carelessly, this phase can doom the entire initiative by

- Marrying it to an unpopular or politically troublesome individual or organization.
- Inadvertently becoming party to unrelated battles for turf and preexisting political scuffles between the new collaborative partners.
- Prematurely constricting the focus, skewing the agenda, or drafting the workplan of the collaboration in response to the narrow special interests of interest group representatives who do not represent the cross-section of actual stakeholders.

Some central principles are at the core of *starting out right*. We should begin by building the core of our collaborations with individuals and institutional representatives:

- Whom we trust and work well with; in other words, relationships we have already built.

- For whom the agenda/problem/need to be tackled clearly and unquestionably overlaps with their missions and self-interests.
- Who are the least controversial within the universe of constituencies associated with the agenda/problem/need.
- Who are of high enough profile and credibility to attract and reinforce the involvement of other targeted partners.

These conditions will allow us to build our initial core with partners who have an affinity for our issue and leadership, are inherently attuned and committed to the issue, and are not likely to limit our ability to attract other partners or predispose the membership and capacity of the collaboration to one particular constituency or perspective.

Remember that we are recruiting collaborative partners to strengthen us, not to repeat us. We are recruiting them in order to build a broadly harmonic collection of voices singing the same tune. This metaphor is an important reminder for all collaborative leaders during our recruitment phase. The significance of "harmony" emerges from its very definition: Diversity is inherent and essential for harmony. Without differences in the timbre and tone of the various participants, we end up with monotonic sound, little more than a somewhat louder single voice.

DIMENSION

Entrepreneurism

Collaborative leaders are always creating, adapting, and innovating in order to establish and maintain their relationships with the individuals (**Interpersonal Entrepreneurism**) and institutions (**Institutional Entrepreneurism**) in their collaborations.

Interpersonal Entrepreneurism: To be effective collaborative leaders, we must use our observations of the psychosocial characteristics of colleagues as tools to shape and direct the relationships we develop with each *individual* collaborative partner. This entails the ability to connect insight and creativity so as to

1. Fine-tune and continuously adjust our relationship with each *individual* in the collaboration to help make sure that each one's evolving self-interests continue to be met and

2. Make the most of every opportunity to lead partners into increasingly productive relationships with the collaboration.

Institutional Entrepreneurism: Our success rides on our ability to recognize and take advantage of opportunities to advance the mission we share with our *institutional* partners:

1. We do the research and ask the questions that help us identify the institutional self-interests of partners (and prospective partners), then develop, evaluate, revise, and refine

the connections between institutional self-interests and the mission and goals of the collaboration.

2. As collaborative leaders, we are, by definition, "out-of-the-box" thinkers. Our approach to problem solving and our world view span the boundaries that constrain most people to persist in looking for solutions within the tried-and-true four walls of their home institutions. Our readiness to straddle borders and step outside the boxes of traditions, norms, organizational constraints, and usual practices reflects, too, our risk-taking temperament and experimental nature.

◆ ◆ ◆

The capacity to be entrepreneurial is even more important for us as collaborative leaders than it is for institutional leaders because our effectiveness in the collaboration derives solely from our ability to build, manage, adapt, and maintain the *voluntary* involvement and commitment of our partners. Let's be direct: If you want to get people to follow you, you either have to own the business that employs them or develop relationships that convince them to voluntarily link their wagons with yours. In public—at least in our democracy—the option doesn't exist to own the enterprise; our ability to lead, interindividually and interinstitutionally, is dependent upon our capacity to build responsive and engaging relationships, to strategically influence and organize others. The opportunity to lead is given to the person whose image and personality are visible and attractive to those who would follow. So it follows that to be effective collaborative leaders, we must develop and employ those people skills and management skills that will increase our visibility and attractiveness in the eyes of current and prospective partners.

Let's keep in mind that, to a very real extent, we understand ourselves only through our reflective interpretation of how others respond to us. That is why a smile or a scowl on the face of a stranger or friend can affect our whole day. If it comes at a moment in which we are ill-formed for the day, it can become our self-assessment. We are not objective; rather we are the results of the external evaluations which we choose to value. The obverse holds too: In general, the fashion in which people relate to us is largely shaped by their perceptions of us. They are not objective either. Their perceptions are shaped by presumptions and physical stereotypes (ask a short person if they don't find people relating to them as being younger or less mature than would reasonably be expected if they were taller), by their prior experiences with people who somehow remind them of you, by their prior experiences with you, and by the signals and messages that you send them at the moment.

As collaborative leaders, we are emphatically aware that our behaviors, and the impressions we make, affect both the perceptions and behaviors of those around us (including their willingness to join in our collaboration). What distinguishes collaborative leaders is that we *take responsibility* for controlling our behaviors and impressions, recognizing that they are the management and leadership tools we can use to build and influence relationships.

In other words, we need to be savvy behaviorists who understand the process of behavior modification and the extent to which our language, style, and behaviors are the stimuli that generate behavioral responses in those around us. Now very few of us have the Machiavellian self-control to strategically plan and execute a regimen of stimuli geared toward generating specific responses in others, and to do so would certainly undermine the humanity and spontaneity of our relationships, which is undesirable. What is important here is the understanding that no one but the collaborative leader has responsibility for the effectiveness of relationships in the collaboration and, therefore, we are responsible for understanding and mastering the relationship management tools available to us. Moreover, if we feel a relationship within the collaboration is beginning to deteriorate, we don't have the luxury of waiting it out or writing it off; it is our responsibility to strategically adapt and intervene in order to repair and maintain it.

Understanding this element of individual entrepreneurism is at the core of effective collaborative leadership. The behavioral exchange or interaction that we've been talking about takes place within our relationships; relationships define the context and opportunities in which we can try to exercise this behavioral influence (this is why we talk of *relationship management* throughout this book). *It is fundamental to an enlightened approach to leadership to understand that we do not manage people, we manage our relationships with people.* Without a doubt, we are influencing (or attempting to influence) partners' world views, interpretations of reality, and choices by negotiating our relationships with them. Fundamentally, relationship management is analogous to the cold-weather game of curling: The best we can do is sweep a path that encourages and makes it easier for the stone (our partner) to move in the direction we desire.

Small business entrepreneurs manipulate the variables of product quality, price, location, service, and so on, in order to accomplish their market goals (and we respect their right to manipulate all the variables at their disposal). We, as collaborative entrepreneurs, intuitively and strategically use our language, behavior, personality, etc. to create relationships that engender confidence, engagement, and support among collaborative partners so as to accomplish our strategic goals.

In general, we can operationalize this and make it easier to think about and do, by asking ourselves routinely, *How do we make each individual partner feel?* Do we make our partners feel valued, engaged, rewarded, important, and enthused or demeaned, superfluous, or taken for granted? When we have the opportunity, do we ask our partners how they feel in the partnership? Do we find ways to discern how they feel about our leadership and style? When such opportunities don't exist, do we do our best to see our relationships in the collaboration through the eyes of each partner? This type of reflection is an important feature of effective collaborations. (See the related discussion below under Dimension: Charisma.)

We've already established that if we understand the self-interests of the individuals in our collaboration, we have a leg up in our ability to build and maintain relationships that they will find interesting and satisfying. There are many persuasive tactics for doing this. For instance, once you find the fire that burns inside an individual partner, that topic about which you simply cannot stop him or her from talking (that is, once they have revealed to you an insight to their obvious self-interests), try to weave that topic into the fabric of the organization; use language associated with it in your description of the collaboration's plans and activities. By doing so, you've woven a piece of the partner into the operations of the collaboration and connected the collaboration more securely to that partner's identity and self-interest.

> On all but the rarest occasions, the relationship is more important than the issue. For the issue-driven outcomes-oriented types among us, this may sound counterintuitive, even shocking. But consider that: (1) It will almost never be productive (in your short- or long-term relationships) to press a partner beyond his or her self-interest in the collaboration and (2) Each of us in our lives will have many issues that we will be addressing, each demanding different partnerships in order to succeed.
>
> If, in the process of cultivating a relationship for a particular collaborative campaign, a prospective partner's enthusiasm wanes beyond repair, he or she gets distracted by institutional or personal demands, or the direction of the campaign no longer conforms to the institutional or individual self-interests of the partner, then it is time to repair to steps of *relationship maintenance*. In other words, don't simply abandon the relationship because it is no longer immediately productive; rather, take steps to effectively put the relationship on hiatus by permitting the partner to graciously bow out of the collaboration without guilt, remorse, anger, frustration, or a host of other possible anxieties and emotions. After doing what it takes to make sure they feel good and comfortable about the communications and relationship they have begun to enjoy with you, you can then file their contact information away to be returned to on a later campaign.

At the root of entrepreneurism are three elemental characteristics:

1. Creativity
2. Willingness to take risks and
3. Willingness to take responsibility.

Creativity is a great unknown: We assume that people either have it or they don't. But, in the realm of leadership, this isn't true. We can learn to be creative leaders.

In large part, creativity is a listening skill; listening, for example, for good new ideas from others, for new insights to partners' individual and institutional self-interests, and for what is not said, for logical approaches that have not been articulated, for holes in logic and conversations that have not been filled. Creativity is, as well, a tenacious resistance to "no" (to the dismissive incantations, "it can't be done" or "it's never been done that way") as an answer. Leaders become creative when they persist in questioning and when they *delay the "no."* Creative institutions can be found where leaders avoid the premature "no," where they operate on the belief that "no" is the answer only after all else has been utterly exhausted, where you find a dogged determination to find a "yes."

Risk-taking runs parallel with creativity as an essential characteristic of entrepreneurial leaders. We must be comfortable and willing to make mistakes and tolerant of mistakes made by others. Without this comfort/willingness/tolerance, we only act when the outcome is a sure thing; and since that can only be guaranteed if the act has been done before, we constrain ourselves from ever moving forward to the new and untested ground where collaborative relationships might take us.

Can a perfectionist be creative? The answer is "yes," as long as perfection lies in the results and not the process.

Collaborative leaders breed creativity by creating environments that permit, support, encourage and value the necessary mistakes that will be made on the road to creative solutions (great books have never been written without an eraser close at hand).

Responsibility, within entrepreneurism, is a straightforward equation: No one but you and me, as collaborative leaders, is responsible for making sure that an answer is found or a problem is solved . . . the buck stops with us. With all our creativity, refusal to accept "no," and recognition that mistakes are steps toward new successes, entrepreneurism won't happen (new things won't be created) unless we accept responsibility for doing them or for negotiating the relationships necessary to enable us to legitimately hold others accountable for doing them. (See the related discussion under the Dimension titled Tenacity and Attention: Institutionalizing the Worry, below.)

DIMENSION

Charisma

Effective collaborative leaders exude a special type of charisma that attracts and sustains the personal and emotional desire of others to work with them.

We should never confuse charisma with dynamism. Charismatic leaders are not necessarily dynamic, although they might be. What makes effective collaborative leaders charismatic is the ability to attract and sustain

Chapter 6

the personal and emotional desire of other people to *want* to work with them—to *like* working with them. It is connected to integrity, dependability, and a general can-do optimism but is really an affective quality that is hard to define and can only be observed—and, therefore, taught—through the eyes of other people. Either people *want* to work with you and *like* working with you . . . or they don't! Those of us who aren't born with the inherent ability to be loved by all have to find ways to see ourselves and our behaviors through the eyes of others. Those "others"—whether they be friends, mentors, coworkers, or other types of "informants"—are the mirrors that enable us to see ourselves, assess our own abilities to attract and sustain the personal and emotional commitments of others, and practice the development of our charismatic skills.

A leader can have all the behavioral self-knowledge and relationship management skills described above under Dimension: Entrepreneurism, but without Charisma this leader is like a lead-footed ballroom dancer with all the right moves and none of the essential grace and believability. In other words, if we give the impression of being driven towards outcomes and fail to get our partners to feel good about our collaborative relationships with them — or if we are viewed as slick, manipulative, intemperate, not comfortable around people or comfortable to be with — then our efforts to be collaborative leaders will fail despite our mastery of all the other dimensions outlined in this chapter.

Charismatic qualities are extremely hard to develop. First, we have to see them: This is the hardest step. We can ask our friends (and even folks we barely know) to help us understand what it is about us that encourages or discourages others from joining with us. We can watch ourselves on tape (like a television reporter) and try to see ourselves as others see us and capture what appears to work in our visual and aural presentations. Then we can learn to imitate certain examples of charismatic behavior which eventually, after repetition, may insinuate themselves into our character.

> Dealing with criticism—as the provider or the recipient—may be one of the best examples of a natural element of our relationships with other people that may cause them to view us as easy or difficult—desirable or undesirable—to work with.
>
> In the extremely rare instance when criticizing someone becomes necessary, the act of criticizing will become a defining moment in our relationship with that person. It can change the temperament and balance of the relationship . . . or it can solidify the relationship by contributing to a shared sense of open and honest communication, by helping to transform incompatible behaviors, and by confirming our qualities as people who lead well and work well with others. Here are some practical suggestions:
>
> Criticism we deliver should always be constructive; couched in the context of both the acknowledged positive attributes of the person being criticized, a clear enunciation of the negative impacts of the criticized behavior, and specific recommendations for remedying the criticized behavior.
>
> As the recipient of criticism we should recognize that in most cases our critic is either uncomfortable or emotionally strained when delivering the message; putting him or her at ease with the good natured and constructive fashion in which the criticism is received will go a long way to cementing a constructive relationship. We should solicit sufficient details so that the criticism is thoroughly understood. Acknowledge the effect that the criticized behavior has or had on that partner. And establish a dialogue with the partner in which recommended remediations are solicited and shared. Discuss a final strategy for resolving the problem. Where possible, engage the relationship partner in the problem solving remediation.

DIMENSION

Managerial Skill

Collaborative leaders are called upon to be effective and efficient managers of their organizations as well as of their collaborations.

This dimension is self-evident, demands little expansion, and is *essential* for the survival and success of a collaboration: We, as collaborative leaders, understand the importance of sound management.

Organizational Management: We ensure that our home organizations are well managed so that we can afford to spend the (often extensive) time needed building and sustaining new collaborations.

Collaborative Management: We make sure that the collaboration itself operates with an air of focused efficiency (in terms of both time and money) and attention to details, finances, and deadlines. We ensure that the cost of participating in the collaboration (in terms of both time and money) never exceeds its obvious benefits from the perspective of *each* collaborative partner.

◆ ◆ ◆

One of the most difficult managerial challenges we will face as collaborative leaders is a human relations dilemma made more difficult by the comparative informality and co-equality of our relationships with partners: *What to do when a partner must be "fired."* Certainly two minds are better than one—that's why we created our collaborations in the first place. But when one mind becomes counterproductive, resistant without legitimate cause for resistance, and drains the resources and threatens the cohesion and survival of the collaboration, then we have three things to consider:

1. *The ground rules that should have been established and agreed to by all participants early on.* These rules should include language describing the proper conduct of—and expectations for—collaborative partners. It's rare that a collaboration's ground rules will stipulate procedures for removing partners (only a very few large and *very* formal collaborations do), but it is appropriate and comparatively easy to build into the ground rules open and routine evaluations of the effectiveness of the collaboration and of each partner's contribution. Invoking these rules should not be too difficult since every partner will have agreed to them beforehand.

2. *Our persuasive interpersonal skills*—our entrepreneurial ability to routinely connect each partner's personal and institutional self-interests to the work of the collaboration—*may have failed.* Either we didn't make the connection for this person, or this person was beyond connecting. At any rate, having failed at this level, it becomes important to save the connection between the collaboration and the *institution* from which this challenging partner comes. (Towards this end, questions to ask include: If there is a higher authority within the home institution, were they aware of the

problem? Can the home institution take responsibility for turning this person around? Is it possible that the resistance this person poses is at the direction of the home institution? Is there an underlying cause for concern in the relationship between the institution and the collaboration? Is there an alternative representative that the institution can send to the collaboration?)

3. The final piece of the puzzle in long-term collaborations is to *establish alternative structures* (such as advisory boards), with nominal and status importance but with no direct day-to-day involvement in the work of the collaboration, to which these challenging partners can be graciously and ceremoniously appointed by the collaboration while their home institutions designate different individuals to serve as institutional representatives to the collaboration.

All this presupposes that we have rigorously and objectively determined that the problem lies in the partner and not in some other—perhaps remediable—element of the collaboration (such as our own leadership or an ill-conceived and dispensable project or direction of the collaboration).

DIMENSION

Timing the Launch

Whether a collaboration is launched in response to a crisis or in order to plan and carry out a long-standing vision, the timing of its launch will influence who comes on board and how best to organize the initiative.

It goes without saying that the process of building a collaborative initiative never happens in a void. Social, political, professional, personal, and (sometimes) even meteorological conditions affect the *readiness* of prospective partners to join and work together: Try launching a new arts and culture collaboration while the national guard is airlifting people from the roofs of their homes during torrential floods!

The collaborative leader controls the *launch* of the collaboration. By this I mean the time and conditions under which partners are convened to begin the process of building the collaborative initiative. The launching is a sensitive and important phase because the convening issue is not clearly defined, institutional relationships are generally undefined, and few if any individuals or organizations have made a commitment to the collaboration as a vehicle for addressing the convening issue (except, perhaps, you as the collaborative leader). At this phase, the rationality of Reinhold Niebuhr's *Serenity Prayer* may guide our collaborative leadership:

> God, give us grace to accept with serenity the things that cannot be changed, courage to change the things which should be changed, and the wisdom to distinguish the one from the other.

In order to time the launch of a collaborative initiative, we need to understand and gauge the implications of the variety of environmental conditions that may affect the outcomes of our efforts. Those conditions that we cannot change we must accept and work around. But those conditions that we can change (by our direct impact, our ability to influence others' perceptions of those conditions, or our patient waiting for conditions to shift, evolve, pass, or otherwise change through natural means) demand our strategic attention.

As convenors of our collaborations, the tools we can use to draw the right people to the table and shape the environment at the time of the initial convening are:

> ➢ Assertion of what power we may have over targeted individuals and organizations resulting from such factors as their trust in our leadership, our position of authority (which may compel them to accept our invitation), or debts they owe that we may call in;
>
> ➢ Our ability to package the presentation of the issue and its environmental context (this is the convenor's equivalent to *salesmanship* and includes marketing, educating, training, and otherwise influencing others' understanding and perception of the issue);
>
> ➢ Our ability to envision our large convening issue in a strategic sequence of realistic and successively achievable stages. This capacity to envision gives us the advantage of being able to realistically estimate (1) what the collaboration will need to accomplish first, second, and third and (2) when we will need to convene in order to meet realistic time frames for accomplishing each successive stage;

- Our simple ability, as the convenor, to choose the optimal time and place of the first meeting;
- Our ability to convey or create a sense of urgency around the convening process. Short but realistic (not arbitrary) time frames are motivators in the right context. And even more compelling is the natural truth that it is almost always easier to organize in response to a (perceived) crisis or against a common enemy.

DIMENSION
Strategic Thinking

The effective collaborative leader is a strategic and logical thinker who understands the steps that must be taken in order to make things happen and who can engage collaborative partners in a productive and efficient planning process.

For very practical reasons, there is a greater demand for efficiency in collaborative ventures than in single-institution initiatives. Collaborations cannot be a waste of time. They must produce product, and they must do so in a timely manner; otherwise partner institutions will quickly see that it makes a great deal more sense to pull back their institutional representatives and have them spend more time on assignments in their home organizations.

Planning establishes the basis for both efficiency and accountability; it is the process of translating into action the shared vision that has drawn the several partners together. This is the purpose of planning. All too often, planning is viewed as a cerebral exercise that simply stands in the way of "doing"—there are countless "plans" sitting on bookshelves, gathering dust, bearing witness to the weak consultants and poor planning processes that produced documents disconnected from the practical context of the organization. When done right, planning is simply the essential and very practical *process of figuring out how to accomplish the mission.*

Planning that is done without direct and routine connection to implementation is not planning at all, it is *authoring.*

Above all else, strategic thinking and strategic planning are anchored in practicality. They push us to set high goals, then to temper and revise them to reflect our practical capabilities. They acknowledge that we accomplish our mission and goals one customer, one client, one constituent at a time. They make the connection between the **big picture** and the **individual constituent or customer** .

The postmaster of the Chicago District of the U.S. Postal Service turned that system around from being statistically the worst performing urban district to one of the best two in the nation by establishing system-wide goals and mechanisms for tracking each late pickup and delivery almost as soon as it happens.[6] The design of *America's Promise,* Colin Powell's national initiative to build collaborative networks of volunteers dedicated to the education and welfare of children in cities throughout the nation, stipulates that local collaborations must be able to track the progress of each and every student *by name.*

---

[6] I had the chance to observe this system work when the alarm was sounded that a bundle of thirteen letters (of the millions processed each day in the district) was not picked up on time. The resources of the entire district descended on the neighborhood station to find out from the individual carrier just what caused the problem.

The effective collaborative leader is a strategic thinker who understands the steps that must be taken in order to make the connections, to make things happen, and to engage collaborative partners in an effective planning process. In this context, our job is to:

1. Translate the vision that worked to convene the collaborative partners into a practical and achievable *mission statement* that is viewed as important, timely and responsive to the individual and institutional self-interests of each partner. This is an iterative process during which the collaborative leader builds consensus around the evolving language of a single unifying mission statement;

2. Move the collaborative partners from *mission* to *action* by breaking down the mission into clear-cut and achievable steps, outcomes, defined tasks, benchmarks, accountabilities that are meaningful, and a process for developing and sustaining momentum;

3. Begin with early goals that are meaningful (though modest), achievable, visible and concretely attached to the self-interest of our partners, and progress to larger, more complex and transformational goals later when the relationships are firmer, interdependencies have seeped into the operations of the partner agencies, and the personal and institutional commitments of the collaboration are strong enough to weather the controversies, conflicts and arguments that may arise as more complex and challenging decisions are made; and

4. Clearly waste no time but, rather, quickly help each partner see *(a)* how the mission will be achieved, *(b)* the benefits of the collaborative

effort, and *(c)* the responsibilities each must assume in order to reap the benefits, prioritize action, and accomplish the shared mission.

Always keep in mind that plans and the planning process flow from the mission. If we want to have the greatest impact on the direction of the group, how it structures itself, who participates in it, etc. then we must make sure that we invest ourselves effectively in the discussions and decisions revolving around the mission statement.[7] Like Archimedes, we can each move the world, with the proper lever: For collaborative and public sector leaders, our mission statements can be that lever.

DIMENSION

Group Process

The effective collaborative leader is (1) an **environmental engineer**, (2) a **group facilitator**, and, all too often, (3) a **grunt operative**.

---

[7] One of the most dramatic examples of this that I've observed took place nearly two decades ago when the Illinois Governor's Task Force on Youth struggled to sort through the range of roles they were urged to play in tackling the "crises facing Illinois youth." This collaboration wound its way through a range of analytic steps in order to find its highest leveraging point of intervention in the "cycle of despair" facing Illinois youth. But, when it came down to choosing its targeted mission—the single lever it would use to most dramatically reverse the crises and break the cycle—this collaboration was moved with persuasion and well-timed and well-honed statistics to the single purpose of reducing unwanted teen pregnancy. They launched the program titled "Parents Too Soon."

If we don't pay attention to the functional dynamics of the group—either by attending to them ourselves or by being responsible for ensuring that other colleagues in the collaboration pick up pieces of this responsibility—then the collaboration will fail. All three responsibilities—as environmental engineer, group facilitator and grunt operative—are nearly always required, although our role as environmental engineer becomes both more important and complex the longer the intended duration of our collaboration.

Our role as *environmental engineer* entails both a body of skills and character traits that enable collaborative leaders to create an environment in which people learn enough about each other to care about each other and to want to help each other—and each other's institutions—succeed. This can be as important a glue as are Mission and Values in getting the individuals who represent the institutional partners to *want* to work together and to be sufficiently invested in the success of the collaboration to make the effort to overcome its many challenges.

This is the element of collaborative leadership that cynics and "Lone Rangers" deplore: Building and sustaining a network of collaborative partners naturally takes more work and, perhaps, more time than tackling the same issue on your own. It also increases the number of stakeholders (those invested in its success) and escalates its profile, impact, resources, and pool of prospective beneficiaries. It demands a conscientious effort to build a climate of mutual trust and comfort, a culture that fosters honest engagement, open communication, and diplomatically couched hardball regarding what will work, what won't, who really ought to talk to whom, when, how, and so forth. It calls, too, for stroking and recognition that reinforce individuals' behaviors and initiatives that benefit the collaboration. Celebrating successes and rewarding contributions are important parts of this process. In bygone days, the testosterone-rich leadership circles of large associations and corporations resisted this type of social engineering, viewing it as soft and unessential, as embracing the maternal characteristics of nesting, nurturing, and launching.

In collaborations, we move beyond this by *celebrating* the success of the collaboration and *acknowledging* the successes of individual partners. This distinction is important for collaborative leaders who, unlike institutional leaders, are in the constant business of building and reinforcing something that exists only by virtue of the collective vision and voluntarism of its participants (unlike institutions with their legalities, structured management and decision-making systems, histories, etc.). Institutional leaders have the luxury of being able to reward and reinforce each individual's performance so as to breed an environment in which individuals strive. We have the responsibility of building an environment in which the power of collective action is recognized, reinforced, and elevated as a driving motive and key to success.

In this environment, interpersonal, interinstitutional and intrainstitutional politics are pretty much left at the door as we strive to make sure that meetings of the collaboration benefit from honest and informed discussion, insights, and action with no fear that underlying political agendas are really at play. Underlying this dimension is our ability to create an environment of dignity and respect. An important tool is our own behavior and role modeling (that is, for example, whatever we may think of the individual character, skills, competence, or even a specific idea of a particular partner, we're obliged to make sure that our body language and other communications convey clear and consistent respect for the individual).

Our role as *group facilitator* entails planning and running meetings, communicating between meetings to help make sure that assignments are carried out, keeping the energy and spirit of the group positive and fulfilling, keeping such politics as may exist (interpersonal and interinstitutional) to a minimum and controlled within our meetings, and so forth. The role of group facilitator is critically important in collaborations since most collaborations do their planning, goal setting, and action steps during meetings of the collaborative partners (whereas most organizations assign elements of these critical decisions to staff or to committees). Each of us, whether serving as chair of the meeting or as one of the several collaborative partners around the table, has a stake in—and a responsibility for—ensuring effective, productive, and well-facilitated meetings.

Some startup collaborations choose to contract-out for meeting facilitators (or recruit outside volunteers) in order to ensure: (1) high productivity, (2) evenhandedness in managing give-and-take during discussions, or (3) to make sure that no one participant has undue influence over the course of discussion. Others establish self-conscious routines for rotating the meeting-management role so that all participants play it equally. The truth be known, peer pressure and the bright light of running a meeting that both involves and is observed by all of our partners virtually reduces to zero the undue influence any one of us can effectively have as the group facilitator. The real hidden influence is the one known to attorneys since the first contract was carved in stone: The person who controls the final write-up of whatever was discussed and agreed during a meeting (the summary, proposal, or draft of language that will be used) can profoundly influence the interpretation, skew and direction of the next steps that will be taken.

Meeting management skills are at the core of our group facilitator role. It's a simple truth that, if the meetings we call are not efficient and productive, we will quickly lose key partners to their other—more productive—responsibilities. Not surprisingly, these skills are more complicated for us than they are for institutional leaders because we do not enjoy the status differential within a collaboration that gives institutional leaders added and immediate authority within their own meetings. In other words, meeting management among people of equal status is different than meeting management involving people from different levels of vertical hierarchies. Teachers and principals, for example, are used to the added clout that status differential gives them in the group activities that they routinely manage. As we shift from our workplace into our leadership roles in our collaborations, we must consciously make concomitant shifts in our mindsets and communications. For example, saying "please play nicely" can almost always be seen as a friendly plea (perhaps from an equal), while "don't fight" will almost always be received as an admonition or threat from someone with greater power.

The following box lists some generic ground rules for preparing ourselves to lead meetings (of one or more people) towards our intended collaborative outcomes.

Ground Rules for Effective Meeting Management

1. *Be very clear just why you are meeting.* What is your targeted outcome? What is it you want to accomplish?

2. *Be alert to all levels of feedback from all corners of the room.* Like actors on a stage, each item of feedback—each stimulus—becomes your cue for a response that is intended to stimulate a desired reaction on the part of your partner(s). You are leading others consciously toward a conclusion (the targeted outcome) and unconsciously toward feeling good about partnering with you. Relationship management is an iterative process: You are the partner whose job it is to consciously reflect upon the stimuli you receive and to strategically control the stimuli you introduce by your reactions.

3. *Master and take ownership of your own management skills.* Don't permit your excellent interpersonal skills to fall victim to ineffectual organizational skills: Learn (for instance) how to run tightly structured outcome-oriented meetings. Understand and build experience in strategic planning, project management, budgeting, and the like. Find the organizational management skills in which you are good and build your confidence in them—build relationships with colleagues who excel in your weaknesses so you can be confident in them.

4. *Ensure your personal mastery of the material at hand.* Even if your contribution to the collaborative partnership is not substantive expertise (if you are, for instance, a policy maker whose contribution is clout in a collaboration built to shape legislation), don't expect the meeting to be a personal tutorial session. Do your homework! Learn enough so as to reasonably equalize the substantive playing field and to ensure a reasonable comfort level in your dealings with colleagues. Nothing will reduce your ability to pay attention to all the interpersonal nuances of relationship management more than having to struggle to overcome the tension created by your personal inadequacy in holding up your end of substantive discussion during the meeting. Understand all you can learn about the subject and your collaborative partners so you can interpret, cultivate, and influence the best contribution each partner can make.

5. *Prepare twice for each meeting.* Always go into meetings with an alternative or backup agenda in mind. This is especially important in the early phases of building a relationship or a collaborative initiative involving multiple relationships because you do not yet have enough data to consistently predict the behavior of the other party(ies) and therefore don't know what challenges might be placed before the primary agenda you hope to accomplish. Always have a bottom line, a minimum outcome, to fall back on (that is, a satisfying outcome that may be less than desired but, still, indicative of progress).

CHAPTER 6

Note that the group facilitator function exposes not only our meeting management skills but our human relations skills for all the world (or, at least, our collaborative partners) to see. How well we can predict, guide, and manage the behaviors of others will predict our ability to facilitate productive meetings. And, as is true in most any context, our skills as group facilitator will nearly always be most tested in the breach—when saboteurs arise to do mischief and to challenge the productivity (and survival) of our collaborations. The box below contains a partial list of what to look out for.

Beware:

The Malicious Saboteur: A prospective partner whose institutional affiliation is appropriate but who harbors—and acts upon—personal animus towards some central figure in the collaboration.

The Limelight Saboteur: Someone who can't function as a co-equal within the partnership but who must be the one whose name, face and title is at the center of the collaboration's public image and internal discussion.

The Power Grabbing Saboteur: Although sharing some common themes with the Limelight Saboteur, this prospective partner will not participate unless he or she controls the power to make decisions. This may stem from either arrogance, a personal need for power, a directive from his or her home institution establishing such power control as a prerequisite for participation, or distrust of the leadership provided by the convening collaborative leader.

The Lone Wolf Saboteur: This person joined the collaboration with no institutional affiliation—perhaps because of his or her expertise, history of attachment to the convening issue, public visibility, or friendship with an influential partner—and weighs in on issues, discussions, and decisions with the same power, vote, and influence as institutional representatives but without the same accountability, connection with practicality, or ability to contribute resources to the work of the collaboration.

continued...

-77-

> ... *continued*
>
> The Ambivalent Saboteur: This *institutional* partner is not fully committed to the mission or process of the collaboration, participates sporadically, and may send different representatives to the collaboration's meetings.
>
> The Sloppy Thinking or Distracted Saboteur: This partner doesn't pay enough attention, reacts only to the immediate point under discussion (often with great passion that diverts discussion in unproductive directions), seemingly is always disconnected or distracted, doesn't know what's going on, is argumentative or makes recommendations devoid of context and with little bearing on the subject at hand, often persists on redundantly returning discussion to the rudiments or controversies dealt with at the very beginning of the collaboration's life.
>
> As a general rule of thumb, if we have (1) built among our collaborative partners an earnest belief that they have a stake in the success of the collaboration (that is, succeeded in connecting the work of the collaboration to their personal and institutional self-interests) and (2) created an environment within our collaboration that both enables and expects direct and honest communication between partners, then other leaders among our collaborative partners will be motivated to help us confront and manage the saboteurs.

Our role as **grunt operative** includes everything from mailing agendas and notices of meetings to doing research, drafting discussion drafts, copying material, and arranging for refreshments. These functions may be assumed by a volunteer or staff person assigned to the collaboration or as a contribution to the collaboration by one or more of its institutional members. But, because collaborations are generally lean operations and are often *ad hoc*, these maintenance and clerical functions that are taken for granted in our offices must be strategically attended to in our collaborations — and that won't be guaranteed by anyone other than you and me.

CHAPTER 6

DIMENSION

Consensus Building

Consensus Building connects the individual and institutional self-interests of partners to the goals and activities of the collaboration. It is *always* beneficial in public sector collaborations for leaders to have the skills to build the largest possible consensus around action before it is taken.

This dimension is closely associated with the group facilitator function of Group Process (above) and draws heavily from the Psychosocial and Entrepreneurial Dimensions.

Some collaborations work well on a consensus model; some survive well by following a majoritarian model. Whether a collaboration takes action only if every participant agrees to the action or acts when a majority of participants vote to take action, it is *always* beneficial in public sector collaborations for leaders to have the skills to build the largest possible consensus around action before it is taken.

Consensus building entails both proactive and defensive strategies. It is the collective product of Individual and Institutional Entrepreneurism that connects the individual and institutional self-interests of partners in collaborative action: This is the purpose of collaboration. It involves the meeting management skills needed to ensure that all options, points of view, and stakes are expressed, discussed, understood, and considered. It entails, also, the ability to keep the collaboration together and active in the face of internal disagreements. In this maintenance role, it is the savvy insights associated with the Psychosocial Dimension and the creativity associated with the Entrepreneurial that enable us to persuade partners who would otherwise go to battle over an issue facing the collaboration to either: (1) find sufficient common ground or view the issue from a sufficiently different perspective so as to reach an agreeable conclusion, (2) find personal and/or institutional value in passively agreeing to a less desirable course of action, or (3) agree to disagree with other partners on the specific action while sustaining their commitment to the collaboration.

In the long run, Consensus Building can be predictable work if the foundation has been effectively laid. One of our first responsibilities as collaborative leaders is to build coalition around both a shared *mission* and shared *values*. If this work is done well—with a clearly stated Mission Statement and Statement of Values agreed upon by every participant as each one joins the collaboration—and if every proposed action flows logically and directly from the Mission and Values, then generating consensus around a proposed action should be a logical and relatively easy process. (Of course, the devil is in the interpretation of just how well connected a proposed action may be to the agreed-upon Mission and Values.)

The foundation for building consensus is laid when we *evolve* a mission that *clearly, meaningfully,* and *simply* connects the self-interests of our partners to the purpose of the collaboration. There can be no ambiguity (no flexibility that allows for undue reinterpretation down the road), the connection must be significant enough to warrant the commitment, and the mission statement should be memorable and compelling, like a slogan.

Meaningful truths are elegantly concise and simple, which is good, since simply stated truths make better organizing tools—symbols around which we can build consensus and return routinely to validate the consensus we have built. Remember our discussion of Alinsky's lesson that the simple stop sign makes a better organizing tool than would the complex challenge of eradicating a neighborhood's rats.

Lyndon Johnson's approach to building consensus is said to have involved gathering his advisors together in a locked conference room, posing the question for which he needed an answer, filling and refilling their coffee cups often, and then not unlocking the door to the bathrooms until consensus was reached. There are, of course, less torturous strategies we can use. But, whatever strategy, five principles should guide our leadership in this regard:

> ➤ *If you can't be clear on the intended outcome, be clear on the question you want answered.* Our job, as collaborative leaders, is to move our group step-by-step toward our shared mission. Even when our best strategies might not be linear, our job is to lead the process that breaks down our mission into bite-size achievable decisions and actions so that the work of our collaboration is clearly directed and productive.

> ➤ *See the world through the eyes of those you would influence.* We cannot find a way to connect our partners' self-interests to a decision until we understand how they perceive and react to the question.

➢ *Tenacity.* There is an adage that the Great Wall of China can be brought down with a ping-pong ball, if one tosses it against the wall time and again until a weakness is found. Our job as collaborative leaders beckons us to be persistent, to push for consensus, and to persist in shaping and adapting the question and the environment until (finally) a satisfying decision can be reached that responds to our colleagues' self-interests.

➢ ***Be an advocate for the collaboration, not for any one decision.*** As collaborative leaders, we are the ones who are most invested in the health and success of the collaboration. And, while our passions may run high on any one question or decision facing our group, we should be the ones to whom our colleagues can turn for leadership and advocacy on *behalf of the whole collaboration.* Collaborative leaders have a duty to be cautious of when and how we advocate specific policy positions or courses of action within our collaborations.

➢ ***When you hit a snag, isolate the objection.*** There will be times when conflicting self-interests among collaborative partners will make consensus seem all but impossible. When this happens, we should take a lesson from sales and negotiation strategies: Ask for and isolate the objection. Narrow the focus of the conflict until it is clearly identified and isolated. Then present the objection clearly so as to ensure its validity for both parties. At this point you may determine that language (the words used to define a position) may be the sticking point. If this is the case, then experiment with language until you can generate agreement on terms. If the objection is more substantial, then establish its linkages to other elements in the transaction: Is the element in question so important to the final outcome that it must be included or can it be simply dropped and, thereby, resolved at no cost? Can it be traded for a party's self-interest that is of lower priority for the success of the collaboration? If so, make the tradeoff clear to at least the two parties involved so that the conflict does not crop up again in another context.

DIMENSION
Professional Credibility

It is important that collaborative leaders be viewed as *credible colleagues*. Credibility is earned by having: (1) **Substantive Mastery**, (2) **Peer Status** and (3) **Professional Integrity**.

The purpose of professional credibility is to validate the appropriateness and generate confidence in your professional colleagues' decisions to join a portion of their visions and reputations with you; to get professional colleagues to invest, first, *in* you and then *with* you at the level you need in order to accomplish a desired purpose.

This dimension was originally titled "Substantive Expertise" until its subjective dependence upon peer and collegial feelings became evident. First of all, "expertise" is not an objective achievement; rather it is a status that is formally or informally conferred by professional associations, educational institutions and peers. Second, in a practical sense, *it is not important that as collaborative leaders we be more expert or smarter than those we would convene*; only that we be *viewed as credible* by our colleagues.

Credibility is earned by having:

1. *Substantive Mastery.* This consists of the baseline knowledge that professionals expect of effective colleagues in their field. Stated otherwise, a professional whose substantive competence is either questionable or an embarrassment to colleagues will fight an uphill battle to gather colleagues willingly around a vision.

2. *Peer Status.* It is generally, and tediously, true that peers must convene peers and, therefore, collaborative leaders must be of at least the same status within our home organizations as those we would convene. Moreover, once the collaboration has been initiated and institutional representatives have begun meeting, it is important that collaborative leaders pay close attention to the possibility of *status erosion*. Status erosion begins when one institutional partner assigns representation to a person within the organization of lower status than the original representative. In some professions and climates, this may produce a domino effect in which the remaining institutional partners react by reassigning and reducing the status of their representatives to the collaboration.

3. *Professional Integrity.* This applies the concept of integrity specifically to the professional context and has a separate meaning of integrity than that described below (in the discussion of Dimension: Integrity). It is measured by codes of ethics, professional standards, and compliance with the principles and normative values associated with being, for example, an educator or an administrator.

It is important to remember that for collaborative leaders, credibility, like beauty, is in the eyes of a fickle and constantly reappraising beholder. If our professional stature is brought into question or if the work of the collaboration falters in a fashion attributable to our leadership; if deadlines aren't met or promises aren't kept and we can be faulted; if a collaborative partner feels that the progress of the collaboration does not justify their continued involvement, then, naturally, our credibility as a collaborative leader is threatened. Beyond ensuring that we strive to achieve the TQM adage of *surpassing customer expectations,* there are at least three routes to protecting and bolstering what we may call this *process credibility*:

1. *Invest in your professional stature.* Make sure you do nothing that could be construed as professionally questionable or embarrassing by your colleagues. And stay on top of your field through professional development, education and research.
2. *Develop ground rules, expectations and benchmarks* early on that establish mutual accountabilities for the administrative and substantive progress of the collaboration. The ground rules and expectations should be adopted by consensus, not by a majority (majority approval means that the fundamental operations of the collaboration have been rejected by a minority of participants). These

ground rules broaden and specify the mutual responsibilities of all partners. In the absence of such assignments, all the work of the collaboration naturally filters back to the collaborative leader. Even with these protections, collaborative leaders are responsible for following up and ensuring that partners comply with the ground rules, accept assignments, and meet deadlines.

3. *Recruit at least one or two highly visible civic or institutional leaders* with high credibility, high status, and in whom you have high confidence that their commitment to the collaboration will result in their sustained and steady involvement. The involvement of partners of this type will go a long way to enhance your credibility and to lengthen the patience of other partners.

DIMENSION

Integrity

At the foundation of integrity are highly effective "people skills" grounded in obvious and unimpeachable honesty, candor, and dependability.

As collaborative leaders, we have to be trustworthy, otherwise our collaborative partners will not be comfortable sacrificing a little bit of

Chapter 6

control over their decision making and public image in order to join our collaboration.

Collaboration is like a marriage with a courtship during which the intentions and integrity of both parties are tested until each is satisfied that a commitment is safe and warranted. Let's explore this analogy a bit:

We begin with an attraction—whether superficial or soul-deep.

If it's superficial, then we can play. But we both are aware that there is little chance that it will last . . . unless we move to deeper substance. Now superficial is *ok*, it can be very satisfying in the short-term (like an *itinerant collaboration*).

Let's assume that both parties find the attraction growing stronger; we both feel that there may be a future, something good to be gained in this relationship. Up to this point we have hidden our flaws and projected our strengths. Now, as we spend more time together, we learn more about each other. If we are not blinded by our passions, we measure each other, do *research* on each other, look for telling missteps and histories that may flag problems or raise suspicions.

At the same time, we judge how the relationship factors into our own needs and future. If we find ourselves believing that the relationship is *good*—that it satisfies both parties' individual needs and fits in just right with our individual visions—then we begin toying with the big question: Does each of us trust the other enough to link our futures through collaboration or marriage?[8]

---

[8] This analogy can continue with relevant parallels to collaborative leadership: *Moving beyond the courtship into the process of building the relationship, of enjoying and* Continued on next page...

Institutional leaders agree to follow leaders they trust. They must be confident that, in the temporary marriage of the collaboration, their trust will not be abused and their decision to join with us will never be a source of embarrassment.

Effective collaborative leaders never compromise on integrity or ethics but recognize that everything else we own or do (language, behavior, even elements of our personality, per our earlier discussion of Entrepreneurism) may be tools to be mastered and employed in our efforts to affect how our partners perceive and respond to us. As public leaders we are challenged to develop and employ the self-knowledge that will enable us to consistently distinguish between those priorities and decisions that we will not flex *(those that define our integrity)* and all our other characteristics that we are prepared to study, grow and flex in order to develop and effectuate the collaborative relationships that are important to us.

At the core of this discussion is an understanding that people who choose to engage in relationships with us (particularly relationships in which we are elevated to some position of leadership relative to them) must be confident in the consistent morality of our behavior and the predictable pattern of our ethics. As public leaders (especially as leaders of leaders within our collaborations) we are each compelled to come to grips with our

---

reinforcing those elements that overlap between the parties and of adapting individually so as to accommodate each other. In this process, which is the ongoing process of both love and relationship management, key benchmarks and events become essential elements around which the relationship is grown (e.g., the first kiss, the engagement ring, the wedding and more are paralleled in events and activities in the collaboration). Of course, separation and divorce are also unfortunate options in this analogy with romance and love—as is reconciliation—which all have their parallels in the course of collaboration as well.

Chapter 6

central defining principles; that is, those values and elements of our character that are central to our identity and self-image.

There is one last point that is especially important for educators and nonprofit leaders. Those of us drawn to leadership in mission-driven public institutions, and especially those of us who would be *collaborative* leaders within this sector, are held by the public and by our colleagues alike to a uniquely high expectation of *consistency* between our mission-related principles and our behavior. The fall of William Aramony, head of the United Way of America, had much less to do with his administrative failings than it did with the lack of consistency between the principles he stood for as leader of the free world's largest philanthropic vehicle serving the needs of the poor and dispossessed versus the values he lived as a freewheeling and high-rolling philanderer.

DIMENSION

Spirituality

At the soul of optimism is the steadfast belief in the righteousness of our mission . . . effective collaborative leaders project this optimism and help us believe it is warranted.

As collaborative leaders, we influence the spirit and world view of those who join the collaboration. On the surface, we are expected to radiate an *energy of achievability*—a can-do attitude—that generates a confidence in those around us that the time they are investing will yield the results we all desire.

At a deeper level, we create within our collaborative framework a culture of coherent values, commitment to egalitarian principles, and belief in the Tocquevillian observation that we accomplish more good together than we ever could alone.

A big part of our job is to establish and elevate a shared vision and to make that vision the touchstone for the work done together by collaborative partners. "Where there is no vision," the Bible cautions, "the people perish." It is up to us to keep that vision vital, to routinely and meaningfully connect it to the individual and institutional self-interests of our partners so that they grow individually and advance institutionally. If the vision loses its vitality—or if our partners begin to view the practical day-to-day character of the collaboration as so different from our organizing vision as to make that vision irrelevant—then the collaboration will perish.

DIMENSION

Diplomacy

Collaborative leaders face the diplomatic challenge of striking a sustainable balance between the interests of individual member institutions and the interests of the collaboration as a whole.

Chapter 6

Of the many bumps in the road that the collaborative leader must negotiate, the most universal and contentious can be the relationship of the identity of the whole versus the identity of the individual member. It is safe to say that few institutional leaders will sacrifice the good of their home organizations for the benefit of an external collaboration. The diplomatic function of a collaborative leader is to strike an ongoing balance between competing and evolving interests. This includes making sure that

1. The collaboration never goes into head-to-head competition with an institutional partner for funding, public profile, or any other significant and potentially threatening element of an institution's identity and survival, and
2. The mission of the collaboration never overlaps so dramatically with that of any one institutional partner as to raise legitimate doubt of the need for both entities.

As a rule, a collaboration's activities should be seen by all participants as the interinstitutional coordination of projects and activities that each partner would have dreamed of doing independently . . . although with less effect. In general, it is risky business for the collaboration itself to have projects and programs separate from those of partner agencies.

Every effort should be made to *illustrate* the degree to which collaborative initiatives integrate and reinforce the efforts of our collaborative partners and to *mitigate* against collaboration activities ever being viewed by our partners as competing for time or financial resources with their own institutions' activities (see the related discussion about the environmental engineer function of the Group Process domain). This principle may work as follows:

1. *New Projects.* When the function of the collaboration is to stimulate or provide a forum for planning new initiatives (for example, projects, advocacy campaigns, and fund raising campaigns) that go beyond the capacity of individual members (or are even designed to extend the mission or programs of institutional partners in some progressive fashion), then care should be taken to adopt new projects only after they have been *(a)* circulated among decision makers in each collaborating institution and *(b)* adopted by *each* collaborating partner as an approved project or program in keeping with their institutional mission. (Other steps that may help ensure broad ownership and comfort with the collaboration's new initiatives include: *(c)* asking partners to show and discuss how the collaboration's initiative fits into and contributes to their own operating plans and *(d)* establishing a budgeting procedure that has each partner formally contribute human or material resources, or both, to the success of the joint initiative.)

2. *Coordination of partners' existing programs or activities.* In many cases, our collaborations serve as vehicles for coordinating programs that individual partners are already offering. These may include coordinating a comprehensive package of social services, linking businesses and nonprofits for community and economic development, coordinating joint purchasing among collaboration members so as to reduce unit costs, and more. In these cases, the role of the collaboration is to be responsive and supportive of the individual

programs and to provide a forum for discovering and exploring *(a)* opportunities for economies of scale and *(b)* opportunities to expand the collective impact of the programs.

A final, inherent quality of our concept of diplomacy is the mission-driven selflessness of leadership. By this I mean simply to acknowledge that effective collaborative leaders spread the credit around among all the collaborative partners for any successes or good decisions of the collaboration. As collaborative leaders, our egos should be attached to the successes of the campaign not to taking credit for them. Throughout the process of building and managing relationships, nothing binds people to a relationship or a process quite so well as evidence that their comments, suggestions, and brilliant recommendations are taken seriously in the relationship and, one way or another, highlighted or actualized in the process of the campaign. At the same time, few things will chip away at the ego gratification offered by a relationship more than the gnawing feeling that one party to it is simply a cipher, rubber stamp, or window dressing in a process dominated and manipulated by the ideas of one other person. No matter how brilliant we are or how dull and uncreative our partners may be, if we have chosen our partners for valid reasons, then our responsibility as the relationship manager is to create an environment in which each partner has good reason to believe that his or her ideas are desired, valued, valuable, and acted upon.[9]

---

[9] In fact, within the collaboration it may well be advisable for the leader to never take credit at all but to dole it out as a tool for building the sense of ownership and involvement of our collaborative partners. (Being publicly credited for something you thought about but didn't do will leave you wondering forever whether you did or said something that had greater influence than you had imagined!)

DIMENSION

Marketing

Marketing is more than publicity: It is the planned and managed dialogue between the collaboration, its stakeholders and beneficiaries, and the general public.

Well-planned and managed marketing should accomplish at least three things:

1. It should project the image and mission of the collaboration clearly and effectively. This both shapes the public dialogue and serves as a touchstone for the collaboration's members; a statement they can return to when they need to remind themselves or summarize what it is they are doing together.
2. It should generate external support for the work of the collaboration in keeping with its mission and goals.
3. It should frame the successes of the collaboration as the successes of the combined efforts of its institutional members (by name) for both internal and external consumption. This tells the story of the benefits of the collaboration, supports the individual identities and aggregate contributions of its members, and helps maintain the collaboration's momentum.

DIMENSION

Resource Development

Resource development is more complicated for collaborative leaders because of our responsibility to enhance the capacity of our collaborative partners and to never hurt or impede their ability to raise the resources they need for their home institutions.

This is a straightforward dimension of any contemporary leadership post but it is more complicated when applied to collaborations. Certainly, as collaborative leaders, we have to know how to find the resources we will need to get the job done from traditional and nontraditional sources, from inside and outside the collaboration. Certainly, this entails skills of researching, cultivating, soliciting, negotiating, reporting, and sustaining monetary and in-kind contributions. The added complexity is hinted in the discussion of Diplomacy above: In the competitive marketplace of corporate, government, and foundation philanthropy, not only is it self-destructive for collaborations to ever compete with any of their members for funding, but collaborations have the inherent responsibility to enhance the capacity of member institutions to meet their institutional goals.

Successful collaborative leaders build a sense of shared responsibility among all the partners for generating the resources needed to ensure the success of the collaboration. When we are successful in creating environments characterized by trust and commitment to the success of the collaboration (see the discussion of environmental engineer under the Group Process Dimension) then it follows that our partners will accept this shared responsibility and will participate in, and contribute to, resource-generating activities on behalf of the collaboration. Once we have achieved this environment of trust, as well as the confidence of each partner that the collaboration serves their appropriate self-interests, then our partners may well tolerate some risk by permitting the collaboration to enter the fray for competitive grants from traditional philanthropies.

Other options available to some collaborations include dues structures, fees for membership services, charging "commission" on money saved through collaborative programs (such as joint purchasing), drawing overhead from grants, and other revenue generated by programs undertaken by the collaboration.

DIMENSION

Tenacity and Attention: *Institutionalizing the Worry*

The collaborative leader is responsible for worrying about the success of the collaboration and for making sure that attention is paid to the maintenance and management needs of the collaboration.

CHAPTER 6

This is, perhaps, the *most undervalued, often ignored, and important dimension* of collaborative leadership. It is the dimension that guarantees that somebody is worried about the success of the collaboration, that the collaboration will not disintegrate for lack of attention. It is a self-possessed tenacity on the part of the collaborative leader: making sure that the collaborative venture is fed, nourished, and attended to during each phase of its development. It is figuratively—if not formally—written into the job description of the collaborative leader or a delegated agent. It is the practical response to the acknowledged truth that if no one person accepts responsibility for the success of any process, cause, project, or collaborative initiative then, surely, it will be displaced to lower and lower levels on everyone's list of priorities until, at last, it disappears altogether. This is especially true in collaborations since all institutional representatives have primary responsibility and loyalty to their home institutions.

Because each partner's priority is with his or her home institution—accomplishing its institutional mission, attending to its day-to-day managerial responsibilities, and ensuring its financial solvency and growth—only the partner whose institutional mission overlaps most extensively with the mission of the collaboration will have the luxury of deciding to expend extensive amounts of personal and institutional resources to support the work of the collaboration. Collaborations that are "staffed" by such a partner agency are challenged to reduce the appearance and fact that the collaboration exists simply as an opportunistic extension of that one partner's own program operations. Short-term *(itinerant)* collaborations, organized around immediate and critical issues can usually succeed as extensions of one credible institutional partner. The challenge arises for *sustained* collaborations in which the ongoing primacy and influence of one partner reduces the co-equal sense of investment, ownership, and responsibility among the other partners.

At the opposite extreme, collaborative efforts that are highly democratic and totally voluntaristic run into their own, often fatal, problem: When no one person is responsible for managing and building the collaboration then the collaboration fails under the weight of its universally second-priority status. Calling meetings, preparing materials, making phone calls, writing proposals, meeting deadlines, and all the other sustaining administrative elements of a collaboration don't get done unless it is in somebody's "job description" to get them done. The best-laid plans and the most fervent commitments made by the most well-intentioned collaborative partners will nearly always be secondary to the crisis, upcoming board meeting, proposal deadline, or staff resignation that occurs within their own organizations for which they are accountable.

One person—with credibility in the eyes of each of the collaborative partners, stature sufficient to deal directly with appropriate personnel in each of the collaborative institutions, proven capacity to administer the collaboration, and a passionate commitment to the mission of the collaboration—needs to worry about (and be responsible for) managing and growing the collaboration. The success of any *sustained* collaboration rests, in large part, on "institutionalizing the worry" in the person of a competent administrative coordinator. Collaborations vary as to whether this coordinator assumes the public role of spokesperson or behind the scenes functionary. In either case, it is this person's competence in planning, managing, and developing the collaboration that defines the collaboration's capacity to make significant progress toward its mission.

DIMENSION
Technological Savvy

Interconnectivity and *instantaneous communication* are the new tools that technology gives us to lead through the power of shared ideas.

At the root of any relationship is communication. Internet technology makes communication spontaneous, easy, accessible and cheap. The Internet:

- Creates the opportunity for us to share ideas with collaborative partners in the middle of the night or while vacationing on separate continents.
- Opens doors to ideas, information, and resources that used to take days or weeks to research.
- Enables us to write together and plan together even when our schedules don't permit us to be in the same room together.
- Puts rules, regulation, and guidelines from government agencies and funding sources in front of us exactly when we need them.
- Enables events planners and meeting managers to find and compare every calendar that might be relevant.

➤ Creates the opportunity for practitioners to *"talk"* with each other, to get answers to practical how-to questions from each other, to find out how others solved looming problems, to find models that have worked for programs that our collaborations may be considering.

➤ Empowers us all with communications resources that we have not yet begun to imagine.

Consider the utility of local networks, in which a number of individuals or organizations are linked together on a local server that permits immediate access to shared space on an *intranet* as well as connections out to the Internet. These enable collaborative partners, individually and collectively, to broadcast and receive information to each other instantaneously. This *intranet* capacity allows, for example, a defined group of users (the members of the collaboration) to share one secure web site consisting of the outline of a project proposal to which they each add ideas and edit the ideas of each other at their leisure from their own PC's and another site on which users anywhere in the world can "meet" at a given time every day to chat (correspond live and interactively online) about the work they accomplished that day towards the collaboration's goals.

Let's explore, for a moment, the most profound—and as yet unrealized—implication of information technology on the world of collaboration.

Begin with the concern, lamented most publicly by John F. Kennedy, that public leaders routinely must make decisions without really understanding all the lives that will be affected, all the implications and unforeseen ramifications the decisions will have (he likened this to the unpredictability of ripples created by a stone dropped into a pond).

continued . . .

Chapter 6

> ... *continued*
>
> Now consider the rapid influence information technology has had on transforming the way we do scientific inquiry. In a very real way, the future of technology may well include the death of scientific method as we know it. The tedious, expensive, and time-consuming experimentation that physical and social scientists do, involving the time-honored approach of testing and proving theses-antitheses-syntheses, is a human creation that reflects the limitations of the human intellect (we can only conceive of so many options, hold on to so many facts, think at any one time in a linear or nonlinear fashion, etc.). The growing capacity of information technology enables virtual and spontaneous computer modeling with which scientists can examine *all* conceivable (and even yet inconceivable) outcomes almost instantaneously. This may very well make the process of hypothesis testing irrelevant . . . and it certainly will enhance public leaders' ability to conceive of (nearly) all the possible implications, interest groups, and organizations that might be affected by—and helpful in—a prospective public project or decision.
>
> With the technology's existing capacity to store and spontaneously share information about individuals and institutions around the world (for example, the work they have done, their institutional missions, programs, scope and resources) and, of course, to open and maintain easy and ongoing lines of communication with them, the door is opening to a future that may include the ability of public leaders and scientists to convene *comprehensive* and *universal* collaborations.

Most of us are light years behind the corporate, scientific, and academic elite who, so far, are the primary users and beneficiaries of this technology. But this technology, and the opportunities it offers, are accessible to just about any collaborative leader in any community in the United States. As leaders, it behooves us to understand the potential of this leadership resource, to be competent with the rudiments of how relevant parts of it work, and to build relationships with those who can help us put this technology to work for our collaborative initiatives.

CHAPTER 7

|A FEW NUGGETS|

This is a book for thoughtful practitioners, so if you are one of those readers who skips to the back of a volume looking for the few nuggets of the most important ideas, let me help you.

The following four principles represent some of the most essential elements of collaborative leadership. They are not a summary, or even a comprehensive overview, but they are exceptionally important. And if you leave this book with only these four points ringing in your consciousness, then (in my opinion) you will be on the road to being an effective collaborative leader.

Principle 1: Develop and refine a common vision or shared goal around which people can rally and find their own self-interests with ongoing renewal and depth of self-identification.

Take your time in clarifying the purpose of your collaboration. Set your sights on a purpose that is worth your while and large enough to warrant the collaborative investment of others. Is your purpose clear and achievable? Is it important (that is, is it a big enough lever to make a significant difference)? Can you explain it clearly (can you sell it) to the collaborative partners you are going to need? Then patiently carry that purpose forward through the iterative process of expanding and refining it until it reflects the interests and needs of those partners you want to bring into the collaboration.

Principle 2: Try hard to see the collaborative purpose and your own leadership style through the eyes of those you would lead.

Through their eyes you will see how to attach their self-interests to your vision and the ongoing operations of the collaboration . . . and you will learn what they need to get out of their collaborative relationship—and out of you—in order for them to invest in the collaboration's success. This demands knowledge and skills that span the boundaries of sector, gender, ethnicity, race, preference and more. It demands the heady confidence to see yourself as others see you, and the will to make adjustments so as to build better and more effective relationships.

Principle 3: The success of the collaboration rests on your ability to build, manage, and maintain essential relationships, one relationship at a time. As collaborative leaders, we are responsible for creating an environment in which the talents, leadership skills, and problem solving capacities of our diverse partners may flourish, emerge, and benefit our collective strivings toward our shared goal. Pick your partners thoughtfully; becoming collaborative partners is not unlike becoming a little married.

Principle 4: Become the *institutionalized worry*. When it comes down to it, if you don't make sure that things get done in the collaboration (from big decisions to routine clerical and maintenance responsibilities), then they won't get done.

Until you hire paid staff, the work of the collaboration will always be everybody's second (or third!) priority—except, perhaps, yours. Every partner is, first, an officer in their home institution, a teacher in their own classroom, a parent of their own children. As central as the mission of the collaboration may become in their lives, we can never count on another to care as much for the success of the collaboration as we do. The buck stops with us (even as the glory will go to all the collaborative partners). So roll up your sleeves and pay attention . . . more attention than anybody else.

◆ ◆ ◆

COMMENT FORM

Please address your comments to:
Hank Rubin
The Institute for Collaborative Leadership
202 South State Street
Suite 1302
Chicago, Illinois 60604-1905
Email: randagroup@att.net
fax: 773/743-0440
phone: 773/743-0448
toll-free: 1/888/NPO-AIDE

Name: _____ Title: _____
Organization: _____
Address: _____ Zip: _____
Phone: _____ Email: _____
Name of most recent collaboration with which you've been associated: _____

Purpose/Mission of the collaboration: _____

Comment: _____
_____
_____
_____
_____
_____
_____
_____
_____
_____
_____
_____

NOTES

NOTES

NOTES